HAL LEONARD

DJ METHOD

BY DJ BIZZON

ISBN 978-1-5400-4956-8

HAL•LEONARD®

Visit Hal Leonard Online at
www.halleonard.com

Contact us:
Hal Leonard
7777 West Bluemound Road
Milwaukee, WI 53213
Email: info@halleonard.com

In Europe, contact:
Hal Leonard Europe Limited
42 Wigmore Street
Marylebone, London, W1U 2RN
Email: info@halleonardeurope.com

In Australia, contact:
Hal Leonard Australia Pty. Ltd.
4 Lentara Court
Cheltenham, Victoria, 3192 Australia
Email: info@halleonard.com.au

CONTENTS

This book is dedicated to my first educator,
my mom, Ms. Wanda Richards-Miller, aka "Diva G."

INTRODUCTION

WHAT MAKES A GREAT DJ

One of my favorite DJs always says, "Know your records." That means love the music you play so much that you know all the lyrics, who produced it, when it came out, its energy level—literally everything about it. Curating a large music collection and cultivating expansive knowledge about your music is half the battle. It will help you learn how to connect your songs and build DJ sets in the best and most creative ways.

TYPES OF DJs

There are many different types of DJs—radio, club, battle, performance, and more. Regardless of where you fit in, your main goal should be learning how to stand out and be original. This starts by learning the tangible DJ skills like understanding your equipment, scratching, blending records, mic control, music preparation, producing your own music, and being professional. And then there are the intangible things like reading a crowd, taking your audience on a journey, and connecting with everyone in the room through the music you're playing. But the most important thing in all of this is to *be you*. Bring yourself into the music. A room full of people can listen to a song and each take something different away from it. What you personally take from the music is what you want to give back to your crowd. These days, everyone has access to millions of songs, but it's how you put it together that matters.

SCOPE OF THIS BOOK

This book is designed for beginners who are interested in learning how to DJ using turntables, CDJs, or a DJ controller with Serato DJ software. It will span topics from equipment and technology to key skills and how to DJ your own events.

ABOUT THE VIDEO LESSONS

To download or stream the accompanying video lessons, simply visit *www.halleonard.com/mylibrary* and enter the code from page 1 of this book. Video icons ▶ appear throughout the book to indicate the corresponding video lessons. Some icons are shown with a time code, allowing you to locate a specific topic within a larger video lesson.

CHAPTER 1: EQUIPMENT & SETUP

There are many different types of DJ gear to use based on your preference, style, and what you're comfortable carrying to your gigs. No matter what type of equipment you use, consider it to be an interactive instrument, not just something that plays songs. Following are the main setups that DJs use, which will help you determine what will work best for you.

TURNTABLES

Turntables are the foundation of DJing. The very first DJs used turntables with vinyl records to play their music. They give DJs the most control over their music and allow you to perform advanced techniques with the highest level of precision. The only downside is that this is the most expensive option.

With all turntable-based setups, there will be a turntable on the left and on the right, with a mixer in the middle. The mixer outputs the music to a sound system so you can hear it.

Turntables and mixer

There are many types of turntables available, but the best ones for performing are those with *high torque*; that is, when you touch or scratch the record, the platter will return to its original speed quickly. If you touch or scratch the record and you can hear it "wind up" to get back to its original speed, it's not ideal for DJing live or scratching. Good options include but are not limited to: Technic 1200s, Pioneer PLX 1000s, Reloop RP7000/8000s, and Stanton ST150s.

If you're not already familiar with all the parts of the turntable, use the images below to learn them.

45 Adapter Holder

Platter

Power Switch

Start/Stop Button

33/45 Mode

Tone Arm Counterweight

Anti-Skating Setting

Tone Arm Rest/Lock

Lever

Tone Arm

Pitch Control

Needle

Target Light

Turntable overview

Power Switch: Knob that twists left and right to power the turntable on and off.

Start/Stop Button: This starts and stops the platter.

33/45 Mode: Determines the speed of the platter. If "33" is pressed, the platter spins at 33-1/3 RPM (revolutions per minute). If "45" is pressed, the platter spins at 45 RPM. Generally, "33" is for 12-inch vinyl records and "45" is for 7-inch vinyl records.

Platter: This is what the vinyl record is placed on while it plays. You should also have a *slipmat*, which goes beneath the record to serve as a buffer between your turntable and vinyl record.

Slipmat

45 Adapter Holder: Some 7-inch vinyl records require an adapter to fit on the center spindle. Any standard adapter should fit into this holder.

Target Light: When pressed down, a small light will pop up. This helps for placing the needle on the record in low-light situations.

Needle: Refers to the headshell, cartridge, and stylus, forming the "needle." The headshell is the top piece that holds the cartridge and stylus. The headshell pictured also has a handle to pick up the needle. The cartridge holds the stylus, and the stylus is the needle-like part that makes contact with the record.

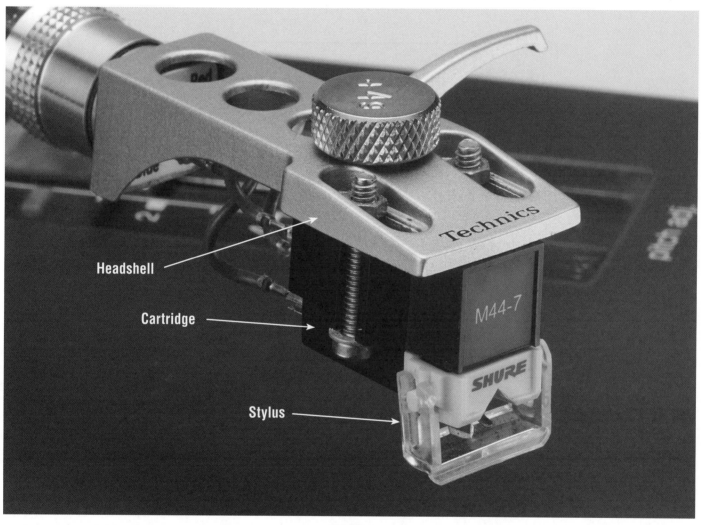

Needle

Tone Arm: Holds the audio cables that connect the turntable to the needle/stylus.

Tone Arm Rest/Lock: This is where the tone arm sits when not in use. A small latch holds the tone arm in place so it doesn't move.

Tone Arm Counterweight: Determines how much pressure the needle/stylus will apply to the vinyl record. The more weight, the less likely the record will skip; however, it will also wear out your record faster. Less weight means less wear and tear on your record, but it will be more likely to skip, especially if the table is vibrating or shaking.

Pitch Control: This speeds up or slows down the record (±8%), which in turn changes the pitch of the song. It is used when trying to match the speeds of different songs.

Anti-Skating Setting: Helps prevent the needle from skipping, or jumping out of the groove, while playing the vinyl.

Lever: Slowly lifts and lowers the tone arm. If you aren't yet comfortable picking up the needle with your hands, you can use the lever instead.

Cables: There are three cables that run out of a turntable. First is the standard power cable that plugs into an electrical outlet. Next is the RCA cable—the red and white audio cable—that connects to the mixer. Last is the ground cable, which also connects to the mixer. Some newer turntables are self-grounded and won't include a ground cable. Note that turntables are *phono* instruments (unless specified otherwise), so they need to be connected to the PHONO inputs on your DJ mixer rather than the LINE inputs.

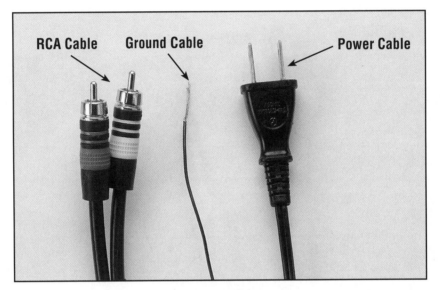

Turntable cables

MIXERS

A 2-channel mixer is the centerpiece of a standard turntable setup. Traditionally, both turntables send their audio output to the mixer, which sits between the turntables. Most mixers have extra inputs that allow you to connect other audio equipment, such as CD players or smart phones, provided they have an RCA connection. There are also 4-channel mixers that allow you to connect and control four different devices at once.

The mixer sends the audio output from the turntables (or whatever you have connected) to your sound system. Newer mixers also allow you to connect directly to DJ software such as Serato DJ or Traktor through a USB cable. Just like turntables, there are hundreds of mixers on the market, so you'll have to decide what's best for you.

Note: The following diagram highlights what's common between all DJ mixers. Anything not labeled is specific to the mixer pictured here (Rane TTM-57) and won't be the same or available on other mixers.

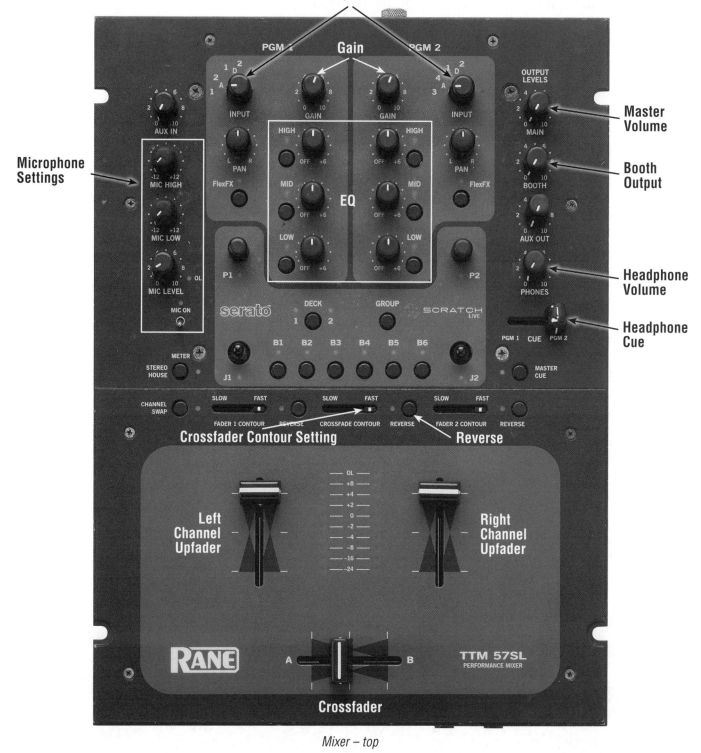

Mixer – top

Crossfader: Allows you to choose which audio output you want to hear. If it's positioned on the left side, you'll only hear the left turntable; if it's on the right, you'll only hear the right turntable; if it's in the middle, you'll hear both sides equally.

Channel Fader/Upfader: These determine the volume levels of each side. For example, if the crossfader is all the way to the left, but the left channel fader is down, you won't hear anything.

Crossfader Contour Setting *aka* "Crossfader Curve": This determines how quickly the volume rises when you move the crossfader from one side to another. For example, if it's set to SLOW, the right side volume will slowly come up as you move the crossfader from the left side to the right. If it's on FAST, the right side will be at full volume the moment you move the fader, even a little bit. In general, SLOW is for playing songs casually and FAST is meant for scratching.

Reverse: This will reverse the polarity of the crossfader. In other words, if the crossfader is all the way to the left, you'll hear the right turntable. And if the crossfader is all the way to the right, you'll hear the left turntable. Channel Faders/Upfaders also can have a reverse option.

Gain: The gain control determines how much electrical signal is getting sent to that channel. The lights on that channel will reflect how much gain is being sent to that side. You want your channel lights to reach mostly the green and yellow. If it hits the red, you're sending too much signal that will result in clipping, or audio distortion.

EQ: All mixers have a 3-band EQ (equalizer) for each channel that allows you to adjust the high/treble (bells and whistles), midrange (the vocal range), and lows (the bass/rumble).

Channel Input Selector: This lets you select which input will be heard on that channel. Most mixers have a "Phono" and a "CD/line" input for each channel. For example, you could have a turntable connected to the phono input and a CD player connected to the "CD/line" input on *just* the left side and switch between them using this knob.

Master Volume: Controls the volume level being sent to your master output. The master output is meant for the main speakers/sound system you are connected to. Generally, this will have an XLR or 1/4-inch cable connection.

Booth Volume: Controls the volume level being sent to your booth output. The booth output is meant for a smaller speaker set up near you or in the DJ booth so you can hear your DJing clearly. The booth and master outputs are independent of each other. Generally, this will have a 1/4-inch or RCA cable connection.

Headphone Volume: Controls the volume level being sent to the headphones.

Headphone Cue: Allows you to choose which side you'll hear in the headphones, independent of what the channel faders or crossfader are set to. This is how DJs cue the next song they want to play. Most mixers also have a "master output" option so you can hear what's coming out of the master output through the headphones as well.

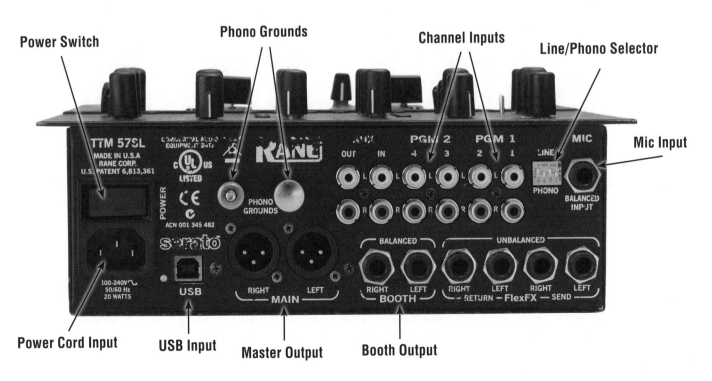

Mixer – back

Channel Inputs: RCA inputs for your turntables. **Note:** On this diagram, "PGM1" is for the left channel and "PGM2" is for the right channel. Two devices can be connected to each channel. So a turntable connected to "1" and a CD player connected to "2" will both be sent to the left channel, and you'd use the Channel Input Selector to control which one is heard.

Phono Grounds: The ground knob is where you place the end of the ground cable. Unscrew the knob, place the end of the ground cable within the post and tighten it. This will ground the turntable and prevent any electrical hum or buzz from being heard.

Line/Phono Selector: Turntables are a phono instrument, so they need to run through a phono preamp to boost their volume to LINE level. So, for this diagram, if you connect your turntable into channel input 1, you need to set the Line/Phono dip switch for channel 1 to PHONO. If you want to connect a CD player or laptop to your mixer, it needs to be set to LINE, since those are already at line level. If your turntable is connected to a LINE input, you'll barely be able to hear it because not enough electrical signal is getting sent to that channel. On the flip side, if you connect your CD player or laptop to the PHONO input, it's going to sound extremely distorted because it's sending too much electrical signal to that channel.

Power Switch: Turns the mixer on and off.

Power Cord Input: The mixer's power cord connects here. Make sure this is plugged in all the way so it doesn't accidentally fall out.

USB Input: This is where you connect a USB cable to your mixer, if it has a Digital Vinyl System (DVS) interface built in.

Mic Input: The input for your microphone. Usually, this input is a 1/4-inch or XLR connection.

Master Output: The audio cable inputs for the Master/Main Output. Generally, this will have an XLR or 1/4-inch connection.

Booth Output: The audio cable inputs for the Booth Output. Generally, this will have a 1/4-inch or RCA cable connection.

CDJs

CDJs are CD players that mimic the functions of turntables so they can be a replacement for turntables if preferred. You load a CD with music on it and manipulate the songs in a similar fashion to vinyl.

CDJ with mixer

CDJs have pitch controls, start/stop buttons, and standard CD player functionality. They also have an RCA cable output so they can be connected to any DJ mixer, just like turntables. Unlike turntables, however, output volume of CDJs are at LINE level so they need to be connected to a LINE input.

CDJ – top

CDJ – back

CDJs are great for mobile DJing, and compared to traditional turntables, have a lot of updated features such as hot cues, looping, pairing with other CDJs, and more. Some CDJs allow you to use a USB hard drive or memory card loaded with music instead of CDs. CDJs can be expensive, with the newest models costing around $2000 each. The only downside is that performing advanced turntablism techniques, such as scratching and juggling songs, is more difficult than on turntables.

THE JOGWHEEL

One major difference between turntables and CDJs is the *jogwheel*. When you play a track on a CDJ, the jogwheel light rotates around the center of the jogwheel to indicate where you are in the song, similar to vinyl spinning on the turntable. The top of the jogwheel is touch-sensitive, so when you press down on it the song stops, and when you take your hand off it plays again.

Jogwheel

Jogwheel Light

Pitch-Bend Wheel

CDJ jogwheel

You can also spin the song forward or backward using the jogwheel, just like vinyl. The side of the jogwheel is the Pitch-Bend Wheel, which is used to "pitch-bend" the song. When rotated clockwise, it will slowly speed up the song and return to the original speed, giving the song a "nudge" forward. When rotated counter-clockwise, it slows down the song and then returns to the original speed.

DJ CONTROLLERS

A DJ controller is an all-in-one unit that combines the features from a turntable and mixer setup with CDJs. So, instead of buying a mixer with turntables or CDJs, you'd only need the DJ controller along with vinyl emulation software (mainly referred to as DVS, for Digital Vinyl System) such as Serato DJ or Traktor. You connect the controller to your computer via USB, and the music outputs from the controller to your sound system.

Pioneer DDJ-SX DJ Controller

Pioneer DDJ-SX DJ Controller – front and back

DJ controllers are great for mobile DJing, as they are generally smaller, lighter, and easier to set up than turntables and a mixer. The price range for the most basic controllers start at around $250, with more advanced units going for $2000. These are great for beginner DJs; however, performing advanced turntablism techniques such as scratching and juggling records is extremely tough compared to using turntables. Also, if one piece of the controller breaks and needs to be repaired, you've lost your entire setup until it's fixed.

USING A DJ CONTROLLER

Similar to traditional DJ mixers, controllers include CDJ-like jogwheels on the left and right side, pitch controls, play/pause buttons, and a mixer in the middle. And since these are used with DJ software, all of your music is stored on your laptop, so you won't need vinyl records or CDs. Controllers include built-in advanced features like sound effects, cue points, looping, samplers, filters, and more. The output is similar to a traditional DJ mixer, as there is usually a master output with XLR connections and a booth output with 1/4-inch or RCA connections.

Every DJ controller will be different, but let's take a closer look at the Pioneer DDJ-SX as an example. This section will highlight the features you need to be aware of and that are found on most DJ controllers.

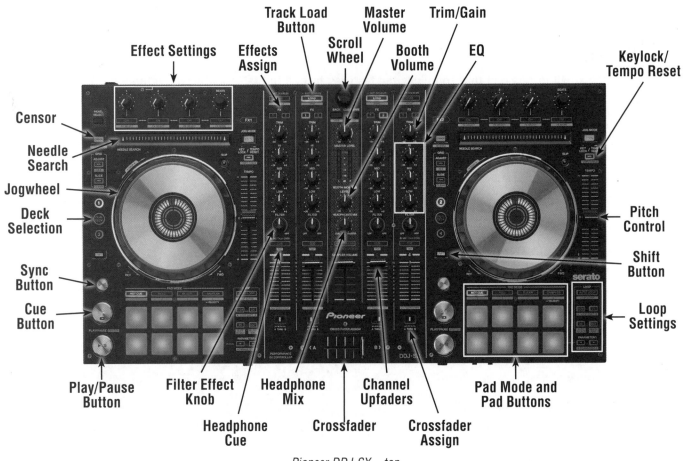

Pioneer DDJ-SX – top

Crossfader: Allows you to choose which side you want to hear. If it's on the left side, you'll only hear the left deck; if it's on the right, you'll only hear the right deck; if it's in the middle, you'll hear both sides equally.

Channel Fader/Upfader: These determine the volume levels of each channel. On the DDJ-SX, there are four channels, with the middle two being channels 1 and 2, and the outer two being 3 and 4.

Crossfader Assign: Selects which side the crossfader will be "on" for each channel. "A" is for the left side, "B" is for the right side, and "Thru" disables the crossfader for that channel. When using the "Thru" setting, that channel will always be on, and you'll only need to use the upfader to control the channel's volume.

Master Volume: Controls the volume level being sent to your master output. The master output is meant for the main speakers/sound system you are connected to.

Booth Volume: Controls the volume level being sent to your booth output. The booth output is meant for a smaller speaker set up near you or in the DJ booth so you can clearly hear your DJing. The booth and master outputs are independent of each other.

Headphone Cue: When pressed, that channel's audio is sent to the headphones.

Headphone Mix: This knob balances how much of the headphone cue versus the master output volume is sent to the headphones.

Trim/Gain: The gain control determines how much electrical signal is sent to that channel. The lights next to your Channel faders reflect how much gain is being sent to that side. You want your channel lights to reach mostly the green and yellow. If it hits red, you're sending too much signal to that side which will result in clipping. When that occurs, turn the gain down.

EQ: All mixers have a 3-band EQ (equalizer) for each channel that allows you to adjust the high/treble (bells and whistles), midrange (the vocal range), and lows (the bass/rumble).

Note: The following list of features only work when the controller is connected to Serato DJ software.

Play/Pause Button: Starts and stops the song loaded on that deck.

Cue Button: When a song is paused, pressing the "Cue" button will set a temporary cue point. So when the "Cue" button is pressed while the track is playing, it will cause the track to restart from that point.

Pitch Control: This speeds up or slows down the record, thus changing the pitch of the song. This is needed when trying to match the speeds of different songs.

Scroll Wheel: This knob allows you to scroll through playlists and song lists in Serato DJ. Press the knob in to switch the focus between tabs in Serato DJ.

Track Load Button: Loads the highlighted song in Serato DJ to that channel.

Filter Effect Knob: This knob applies either a high-pass filter or low-pass filter to the channel depending on which way it's turned.

Censor: When held down, it will temporary play the track in reverse as a way to censor explicit words. When the button is lifted, the track will continue as if the censor had not been pressed.

Needle Search: Using your finger, this allows you to quickly scroll through the track that is loaded on the deck.

Jogwheel: The jogwheel mimics the function of a turntable and allows you to manipulate the track that's loaded. The jogwheel light rotates around its center to indicate where you are in the song, similar to vinyl spinning on the turntable. The top of the jogwheel is touch-sensitive, so when you press down on it, the song stops, and when you take your hand off, it plays again. You can also spin the song forward or backward using the jogwheel, just like vinyl. The side of the jogwheel is the Pitch-Bend Wheel, which is used to "pitch-bend" the song. When rotated clockwise, it will slowly speed up the song and return to the original speed, giving the song a "nudge" forward. When rotated counter-clockwise, it slows down the song and then returns to the original speed.

Deck Selection: The DDJ-SX has four input channels, and the deck selection button allows you to switch between Decks 1 and 3 on the left side and Decks 2 and 4 on the right side.

Sync Button: Turns on the Serato DJ Sync feature for that deck. To assist with mixing songs, it automatically matches the BPMs of the tracks to each other.

Keylock/Tempo Reset: Keylock will lock the original key of the song even when the pitch is adjusted. Tempo Reset sets the pitch control of that deck to zero regardless of where the pitch control slider is set.

Shift Button: When held down, this enables secondary features of various buttons on the controller.

Pad Mode and Pad Buttons: This selects and enables various effects such as Cue Points, Loop Rolls, the Slicer, and the Sampler.

Effects Assign: Determines which effects bank will be applied to that channel. Both can be selected at once.

Front

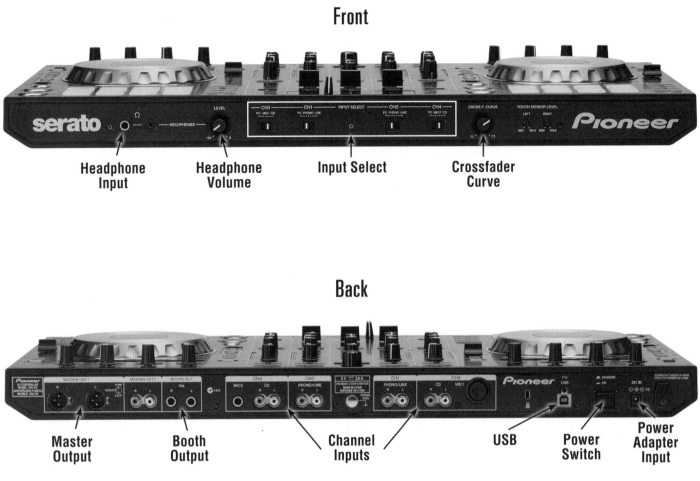

Pioneer DDJ-SX DJ Controller – front and back

Headphone Input: 1/4-inch and 1/8-inch inputs for headphones.

Headphone Volume: Controls the volume of your headphones.

Input Select: Similar to the Input Selector on a traditional mixer, this lets you select which input will be heard on that channel. On the Pioneer DDJ-SX, the options are PC (the song loaded in Serato DJ on that channel), Mic1, Mic2, Phono/Line, or CD. **Reminder:** PHONO is for turntables, and LINE is for items like CD players, phones, DVD players, etc.

Crossfader Contour Setting *aka* "Crossfader Curve": This determines how quickly the volume rises when you move the crossfader from one side to another. For example, if it's SLOW, the right side volume will come up slowly as you move the crossfader from the left side to the right. If it's FAST, the right side will be at full volume the moment you move the fader, even a little bit. SLOW is generally used when playing songs casually, and FAST is meant for scratching.

Master Output: The audio cable inputs for the Master Output. On the Pioneer DDJ-SX, it has an XLR and RCA cable connection.

Booth Output: The audio cable inputs for the Booth Output. On the Pioneer DDJ-SX, it has a 1/4-inch connection.

Channel Inputs: The Pioneer DDJ-SX allows you to connect other audio devices to the controller, including microphones, turntables, CD or DVD players, and smart phones.

Power Switch: Turns the controller on and off.

Power Adapter Input: The mixer's power cord connects here. Make sure this is plugged in all the way so it doesn't accidentally fall out.

USB Input: To connect the USB cable from your computer.

VINYL EMULATION SOFTWARE

Most DJs now use software that lets them play music on their computer through their DJ setup. The two most popular options are Serato DJ and Traktor. They are available to download for free, but you'll need Serato-enabled or Traktor-enabled hardware connected to your computer to unlock all of the live DJing features. Without anything connected, you can still import music, create playlists, and use other features like setting cue points and loops.

The hardware can either be a stand-alone interface that connects your mixer to your computer, a DJ mixer with the interface built in, or a DJ controller like the Pioneer DDJ-SX. All of them require a USB connection to your laptop. Examples of stand-alone interfaces are the Rane SL series or the Traktor Audio series. Popular Serato-enabled DJ mixers are the Rane 62, Rane 72, Pioneer DJM-S9, and Pioneer DJM-900.

Rane SL1 stand-alone interface

Denon DJ DS1 stand-alone interface

Pioneer DJM-S9 mixer

Rane 72 mixer

Once you connect the hardware, virtual DJ decks will appear on the software display on your laptop screen, and with specialized vinyl or CDs, you can play and manipulate songs using your turntables, CDJs, or DJ controller. When connected, the audio will then come out of your hardware, not your computer.

The biggest advantage of using DJ software is that instead of having to haul around hundreds of records or CDs, you just need your laptop. DJ software also includes features like auto-BPM detection, cue points, loops, effects, and more built into it. This makes it easy for DJs to keep their music organized and be prepared for all different types of events with ease.

The largest disadvantage is that you need a very reliable computer to run DJ software, which means spending more money. Sometimes computers crash or malfunction, and if you don't have a backup, you could be out of luck. So if you go this route, make sure you have a computer that you trust and that you have your music backed up on multiple external hard drives.

This book will focus on using Serato DJ software. A full description of Serato DJ, along with download instructions, keyboard shortcuts, minimum requirements for your computer, and features list can be found at *www.serato.com*. Below are the main features in Serato DJ that you need to be aware of when no Serato-enabled hardware is connected. Even without any hardware connected, DJs use Serato DJ to listen to music, organize their crates, and plan sets in advance.

Serato DJ main screen with playlists

Song List: Shows the complete list of songs that have been imported into Serato. Songs can be added using the "Files" button or by simply dragging individual songs or folders into Serato DJ.

Playlists: This shows all playlists, *aka* "Crates," that have been created. The button with the "+" symbol and orange box allows you to create new playlists. "Smart" playlists can be created by hitting the button with the "+" symbol and blue box.

Track Display: This area shows all of the song information. To load a song, simply drag a song onto the Track Display area. Use the "Play" button to play and pause the song. The keyboard shortcut for "Play/Pause" is the space bar. This area is also where you can set cue points and loops.

Cue Points: These let you immediately jump to a certain part of a song that you set yourself. You get eight cue points per track. **Note:** When you hit a cue point on a DJ controller with a jogwheel light, it will automatically reset the jogwheel light facing up. This lets you visually see on your controller where the cue point is instead of having to look at your computer screen.

Loops: Loops replay a short section of a song until the loop is turned off. You can set loops manually or automatically and save up to eight loops per song.

Waveform Display: This is the audio waveform of the song loaded. You can click and drag the waveform forward and backward to move around in the song.

Analyze Files Button: This will analyze every song in your library to determine BPM (beats per minute, or tempo), key, length, and bitrate.

Search: Allows you to search for songs in the selected playlist.

Column Names: You can sort your music based on the column header by simply clicking the column name. Right-clicking on the column header will show all the available columns that can be viewed and if they are visible or not.

Autoplay: When highlighted, as one song ends, the next song in the list will play automatically. If not highlighted, once the track that is playing ends, it will just go to silence.

Master Output: Knob and indicator light for the Master Output of Serato DJ.

Help: When pressed, various help options are available to assist in using Serato DJ.

Settings: When pressed, the Settings tabs open so you can customize Serato DJ to your liking.

SERATO DJ WITH SERATO-ENABLED HARDWARE CONNECTED

When you connect a Serato-enabled device to your computer, the "Virtual Decks" appear in Serato DJ.

Serato DJ with Virtual Decks

The "Virtual Decks" shows the BPM of the song, pitch, pitch range, elapsed time, remaining time, the platter position indicator, and the track progress indicator. This allows you to visually see exactly what's happening with your music and what the settings are on your turntables, CDJs, mixer, or DJ controller.

SPEAKERS

No matter what type of gear you buy, you'll need to connect it to speakers to hear the music. Some gigs will already have speakers or a sound system available to use. But if you're a mobile DJ or doing events on your own, you'll need to provide them yourself.

Just like DJ gear, there are many options when it comes to speakers. You'll need speakers that:

- are loud and powerful enough for the spaces you're playing.

- are within your budget.

- you're able to carry or use with a dolly for transport.

Most mobile DJs will have a pair of powered speakers and a powered subwoofer. Powered speakers cost more, but they don't require an amplifier and can be plugged into a regular power outlet. Unpowered, or "passive," speakers are much cheaper and don't need to be plugged in to a power outlet, but they do require a powered amplifier to boost the sound. With either type, ideally you'll place them on stands to the left and right of your setup, with the subwoofer placed on the floor.

QSC K12 powered speaker – front and back

Speakers on stands

CABLES

The music comes out of your mixer or DJ controller through an audio port. You'll need to connect a cable from that output port to the input port on your speakers. Most DJ gear has three different types of audio ports: RCA, 1/4-inch, or XLR. Make sure that whatever audio port your DJ gear has is the same as your speakers/sound system. If not, you'll need to buy different speakers or get conversion adapters for your cables.

For example, if your DJ controller has an RCA output but your speakers only have 1/4-inch inputs, you can purchase RCA-to-1/4-inch adapters to make the connection. Or you can buy a cable that has RCA terminals on one end and 1/4-inch terminals on the other.

Another common cable you'll run into are 1/8-inch cables, which are the size of traditional headphone ports. Most DJ gear actually has 1/4-inch *and* 1/8-inch inputs for headphones. But if your DJ gear doesn't have an 1/8-inch input, you'll need an 1/8-to-1/4 adapter.

RCA cable   XLR cable   1/4" cable

RCA to 1/4" cable   1/8" to 1/4" adapter   RCA to 1/4" adapters

WHAT SHOULD YOU BUY?

The DJ gear that you choose will depend on two main things: 1) the type of DJ you want to be, and 2) your budget. If you want to be a very technically skilled DJ that can perform advanced techniques, then save up to buy turntables. If you are more interested in being a party-rocker or a mobile DJ, then go for a DJ controller and/or CDJs. And if you do want a traditional turntable setup but can't afford it, start with a DJ controller and over time work your way up to turntables.

No matter what gear you use, just be creative. **Max out the creativity on your equipment, whatever it is.** If you have a beginner DJ controller, as you progress, there will come a point where you run out of things to do with it, and that's when you'll need to step up to a more advanced controller or turntables. As long as you have a passion for music and continue to improve, you'll be fine.

CHAPTER 2: SETTING UP & TURNING ON GEAR

 In this section, we'll cover setting up turntables with a mixer, CDJs with a mixer, and a DJ controller. With each of these, the first thing you need to do is simply clear off a table or a long flat space. Next, make sure you have enough power outlets for all your equipment. You'll probably need a power strip with a surge protector. Finally, make sure all power buttons are in the OFF position and all your volume levels and faders are turned all the way down.

POWER-UP SEQUENCE

Before setting up the gear, you must first learn the order in which you should turn sound equipment on and off. The simple way to think of it is to turn on everything in the order from where sound begins to where sound ends. It may seem trivial, but this is essential to protect your gear. For example, if you turned the speakers on first and then turned on your mixer with the volume all the way up, you could damage your speakers.

DJ EQUIPMENT POWER-UP SEQUENCE:

1. Turntables, CDJs, or DJ Controller

2. Mixer

3. Amplifier (if needed)

4. Sound System/Speakers

And when it's time to power down, simply do so in the opposite order; that is, turn your DJ equipment off in order from where sound ends to where sound begins. Again, doing so will help protect your gear. Sometimes when turning off DJ equipment like turntables or a mixer, residual electricity will flow through the audio cables to the speakers, resulting in a loud pop if the speakers are on, which could damage them.

DJ EQUIPMENT POWER-DOWN SEQUENCE:

1. Sound System/Speakers

2. Amplifier (if needed)

3. Mixer

4. Turntables, CDJs, or DJ Controller

SOUND FLOWCHART

Below is the flowchart of how sound travels through your DJ equipment and the four main ways you can adjust the volume of your DJ setup. Use this as your guide to set your volume at each step. A bad signal at any step will continue down the line making everything sound bad, so make sure you have a clear signal throughout.

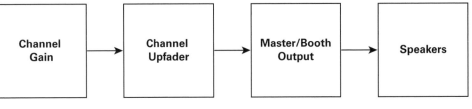

Sound flowchart

Channel Gain: The gain for each channel on the mixer is the amount of electrical signal being sent to that channel. Too much channel gain will cause the sound coming out of the channel to distort, thus making it distort everywhere down the line. Too little gain will cause the sound to be weak coming out of the channel, thus making it sound quiet everywhere down the line. Usually the channel gain knob can be left facing up (12 o'clock). The channel lights should bounce between green and yellow. If it hits the red, your sound is distorting, so turn the channel gain down. If both songs on the left and right deck are near the same channel light levels, that usually means they are both the same volume.

Channel Upfader: The channel faders control the range of the channel gain, starting and ending from no sound to whatever the gain is set to. Use the channel upfader to adjust the volume or balance out the volumes of each song on the left and right deck. Keep in mind that the channel upfader *does not change* the channel gain.

Master/Booth Output: This is the main output of your mixer that combines the balance of the channel faders and the crossfader to determine what gets sent to the speakers. If the crossfader is on either the left or right side, it will output just that side. If it's in the middle, it will output both sides. Having the master/booth output set too high can overload your speakers, so set this at a reasonable volume. Most DJ mixers/controllers have a master output light as well. So, similar to the channel gain lights, keep the Master/Booth output lights bouncing between green and yellow.

Speakers: Your speakers will have their own volume control to set. After everything else is set properly, you can then adjust your speaker volume. If your sound is distorting but your speaker volume is low, you might be sending too much signal to your speakers. In that case, turn down the Master/Booth output on your mixer/DJ controller. On the flipside, if your speaker volume is really loud but it's not turned up that high, turn down your mixer master volume.

TURNTABLES AND A MIXER

Let's take a look at a DJ setup using turntables and a mixer.

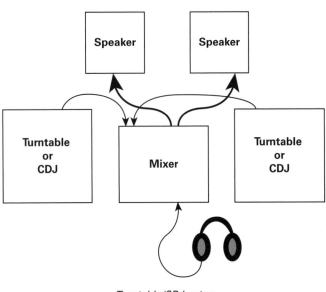

Turntable/CDJ setup

1. Place the two turntables and mixer on a flat surface. Make sure everything is at a comfortable height. Your arms and hands should rest flat on the mixer and turntables.

2. Make sure the power buttons on the turntables, mixer, and speakers are in the OFF position.

3. Place the mixer between the turntables as shown in the previous diagram.

4. Plug the turntable's RCA cables into the PHONO inputs on the back of the mixer. There should be one for the left channel and one for the right.

5. Lightly unscrew the ground knobs on the back of the mixer, insert the tip of the turntable ground cables into the space, and screw the knob back in. If your mixer only has one ground knob, use both ground cables on the one knob.

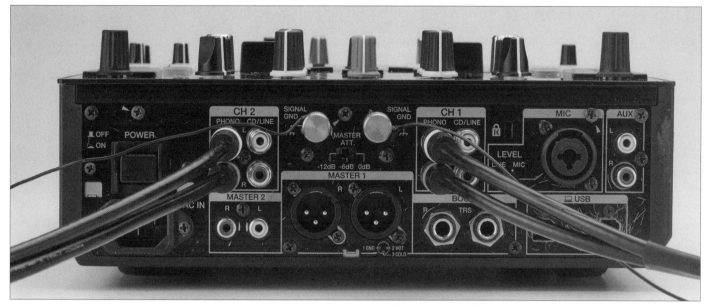

Connecting RCA cables and ground wires to the mixer

6. Insert the needles into the sockets on the turntable tone arm and screw them in tight.

Connect turntable needle

7. Place slipmats directly onto the platters.

8. Grab two records, make sure they're clean (wipe with a soft cloth if necessary), and place them on top of the slipmats.

9. Connect your mixer to your speakers using the requisite audio cables for your setup.

10. Plug the power cables for the turntables, mixer, and speakers into power outlets (or a power strip).

11. Turn everything on in the correct order: Turntables > Mixer > Speakers.

12. On your mixer, make sure your Channel Input Selector for both the left and right channel is set to PHONO/VINYL.

CDJs AND A MIXER

Now let's check out the proper setup using CDJs and a mixer.

1. Place two CDJs and a mixer on a flat surface. Make sure everything is at a comfortable height. Your arms and hands should rest flat on the mixer and CDJs.

2. Make sure the power buttons on the CDJs, mixer, and speakers are in the OFF position.

3. Place the mixer between the CDJs.

4. Plug the CDJ's RCA cables into the LINE inputs on the back of the mixer. There should be one for the left channel and one for the right.

5. Connect the mixer to the speakers using the appropriate audio cables for your setup.

6. Plug the power cables for the turntables, mixer, and speakers into power outlets (or a power strip).

7. Turn everything on in the correct order: CDJs > Mixer > Speakers.

8. On your mixer, make sure your Channel Input Selector for both the left and right channels is set to CD/Line.

SERATO DJ INTERFACE

If you have a stand-alone Serato DJ DVS Interface, your setup will look like this:

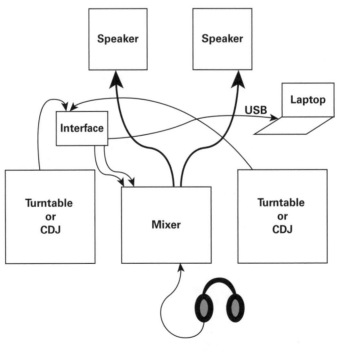

Turntable/CDJ with DVS interface setup

First, you'll connect your turntables/CDJs to the left and right input channels on the DVS interface itself. Then the left and right channel outputs of the DVS interface are sent to the LINE input of your mixer. Your DVS interface will also have a USB cable that you will need to connect to your computer. If the DVS interface is built into your mixer, just plug your turntables/CDJs into your mixer like normal, but make sure the Channel Input Selectors are set to PC. Your computer will probably need drivers installed for your DVS Interface, so if prompted, download and install the necessary drivers. After this, you may have to either restart Serato DJ or your computer as well.

Once everything is installed, and Serato DJ is open, plug the USB from the DVS interface into your computer. After a few moments, the Virtual Decks should appear on your screen indicating that your DVS interface is connected properly. Make sure to import the music that's on your computer into your DJ software. You can drag and drop your music files or folders right into Serato DJ.

DJ CONTROLLER

Here's the setup when using a DJ controller.

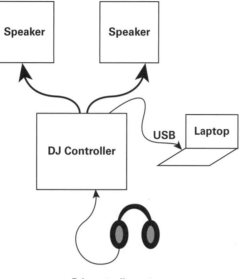

DJ controller setup

1. Place the DJ controller on a flat surface. Make sure everything is at a comfortable height. Your arms and hands should rest flat on the controller.

2. Make sure the power buttons on the DJ controller and speakers are in the OFF position.

3. Connect the DJ controller to your computer using the USB cable.

4. Plug all power cables into power outlets (or a power strip).

5. Download, install, and open Serato DJ on your computer.

6. Turn on your DJ controller. Your computer will probably need drivers installed for it. If prompted, download and install the necessary drivers. After this, you may have to either restart Serato DJ or your computer.

7. After a few moments, the Virtual Decks should appear on your screen indicating that your DJ controller is connected properly.

8. Make sure to import the music that's on your computer into your DJ software. You can drag and drop your music files or folders right into Serato DJ.

9. Turn on your speakers.

10. On your controller, make sure your Channel Input Selector for both the left and right channels is set to PC.

CHAPTER 3: PLAYING (WITH) MUSIC

 Now that everything is powered up, it's time to play some music. In this chapter, we'll go over how to do this with vinyl records, CDJs, and DVS software.

TURNTABLES

If you're using turntables with vinyl records, here's the step-by-step process to get you started.

1. Make sure your records are clean by wiping them off with a soft cloth.

2. Place a record on the left turntable. (Make sure you have a slipmat down first.)

3. Lift the tiny latch (tone arm lock) up with your thumb to release the tone arm.

4. Lift the needle by the handle off the rest and softly drop the needle at the outer edge of the record. Records spin clockwise and play from outside to inside. Always pick the needle up by the handle and not by the cartridge or the tone arm.

Unlocking the tone arm latch with thumb

Grabbing the needle handle

Putting the needle down on the record

5. Hit play on the left turntable to play the record. Set the crossfader all the way to the left and push the left upfader all the way up.

6. Make sure the gain knob on the left channel and the master volume on your mixer are both up. A good place to set them for now (along with your EQ knobs) is facing up, or in the 12 o'clock position. Even with the speakers currently off or turned down, you should see lights on your left channel and master channel showing that a signal is going through the channels. Adjust the channel gain and master gain so the lights stay in the green and yellow. If either is in the red, turn it down.

7. Now, turn your speakers up to a comfortable level. You should hear music coming out of the speakers. Just listen to the music for a minute or so.

8. Grab a different record and play a song on the right turntable.

9. Use the channel fader to control the volume of the right channel turntable and use the crossfader to choose which turntable you want to hear.

10. Get comfortable touching the record and listening to different parts of the record. Do this by picking up the needle (by its handle) and placing it at different parts of the record. When moving the needle, do not drag the needle across the record. You can damage your record and needle this way. When this happens, you'll hear a loud scratch sound, so do your best to prevent this.

11. Also, with your hand, spin the record clockwise and counter-clockwise. When spinning the record, make sure to place your hand on the inside of the record so that you don't accidentally hit the needle.

Proper hand placement for clockwise spinback

Proper hand placement for counter-clockwise spinback

12. In general, keep your hand on the left side of the record on either turntable so that your hand doesn't hit the needle.

13. Vinyl records have 5–8 second pauses between songs, which you can see as thin, dark paths of empty space on the record. Practice placing the needle directly onto all the empty spaces while listening to the songs on your record.

Close-up of space between songs

14. Connect a pair of headphones to your mixer and listen to music solely in the headphones. Turn the channel faders down and get comfortable switching between the left and right turntables with the headphones on.

15. Keep the headphone volume reasonable to prevent ear damage.

ACTIVITY

Spend 15–30 minutes just listening to different records. Get comfortable putting new records on each side, picking up the needle properly, moving the tone arm, adjusting the pitch control, using the EQ, and just becoming familiar with your equipment.

TROUBLESHOOTING

If your music is not playing or is really quiet, use this checklist to troubleshoot:

- Make sure all your cables are firmly plugged in between the turntables and mixer and from the mixer to the speakers.

- Check the On/Off switches for all the equipment and make sure everything is ON.

- Make sure your speakers are turned up.

- Unscrew and reattach your needles to your tone arm. Make sure you firmly tighten them in.

- Check the Channel Input Selector knob on your mixer and make sure it's set to the correct input, based on which input your turntables are connected to in the back of the mixer.

- Make sure the turntables are connected to the PHONO input in the back of your mixer. Or if there is a PHONO/LINE switch for that channel, set it to PHONO. If it's set to LINE or in a LINE input, the volume will be very low no matter how much you turn it up.

- If you hear a buzzing or humming noise coming from either turntable, your ground wire might not be connected correctly, so reattach it to the ground post.

- If you still can't hear anything, you may have faulty equipment that needs to be repaired.

USING SERATO DJ WITH TURNTABLES

As a reminder, Serato DJ can be used with a traditional turntable setup. If you have a Serato DJ-enabled interface, follow the instructions that came with it to incorporate it into your turntable setup. Then follow the previous steps to start playing music.

CDJs

For those of you using CDJs, follow these steps:

1. On the left CDJ, insert a CD with music. If your CDJ allows thumb drives or SD cards with music to be connected, you can use that instead of a CD. After a few moments, the track list should show up on the screen.

2. Use the scroll wheel to select the track you'd like to hear.

3. Push the scroll wheel in and the highlighted song will load.

4. Hit play on the left CDJ to play the track. Instead of the platter spinning, you'll see the light in the center of the jogwheel spin clockwise. Position the crossfader all the way to the left side and slide the left upfader all the way up.

5. Make sure the gain knob on the left channel and the master volume on your mixer are both up. A good place to set them for now (along with your EQ knobs) is facing up, or in the 12 o'clock position. Even with the speakers currently off or turned down, you should see lights on your left channel and master channel showing that a signal is going through the channels. Adjust the channel gain and master gain so the lights stay in the green and yellow. If either is in the red, turn it down.

6. Now, turn your speakers up to a comfortable level and just listen to the music for a minute or so.

7. Grab a different CD and play a song on the right CDJ.

8. Use the channel fader to control the volume of that channel's CDJ and use the crossfader to choose which side you want to hear.

9. Get comfortable touching the jogwheel to play and pause the track with your hand. Also, spin the jogwheel clockwise and counter-clockwise to move around in the song.

10. To use the pitch-bend feature, rotate the sides of the jogwheel clockwise and counter-clockwise. If done correctly, this will speed up or slow down the song while rotating and then return to the original speed when released. It shouldn't stop the music.

11. Skip to different tracks using the "Track Search" buttons or the scroll wheel.

ACTIVITY

Spend 15–30 minutes just listening to different CDs. Get comfortable putting new CDs into each CDJ, using the jogwheel, adjusting the pitch control, using the EQ, and just getting familiar with your equipment.

TROUBLESHOOTING

If your music is not playing, or if it's distorted, use this checklist to troubleshoot:

- Make sure all your cables are firmly plugged in between the CDJs and mixer and from the mixer to the speakers.

- Check the On/Off switches for all the equipment and make sure everything is ON.

- Make sure your speakers are turned up.

- Check the Channel Input Selector knob on your mixer and make sure it's set to the correct input, based on which input your CDJ is connected to in the back of the mixer.

- Make sure the CDJs are connected to the LINE input in the back of your mixer. Or if there is a PHONO/LINE switch, set it to LINE. If it's set to PHONO or in a PHONO input, the volume will be extremely distorted no matter much you turn it down.

- If you still can't hear anything, you may have faulty equipment that needs to be repaired.

USING SERATO DJ WITH CDJs

As a reminder, Serato DJ can be used with a traditional CDJ setup. If you have a Serato DJ-enabled interface, follow the instructions that came with it to incorporate it into your CDJ setup. Then follow the previous steps to start playing music.

DJ CONTROLLER WITH SERATO DJ

If you followed the setup steps in Chapter 2, you should have Serato DJ software open on your computer, and the Virtual Decks should be visible on your screen. We will use the Pioneer DDJ-SX as the example controller for this section.

1. Click and drag a song from your song list directly onto the left virtual deck. Or you can use the scroll wheel to highlight the song you want to use and hit the "Load" button on channel 1.

2. Hit the left deck's play button. Make sure the crossfader is all the way to the left and the channel 1 fader is all the way up. You should see the channel lights brighten up, indicating everything is properly connected.

3. Make sure the gain knob on the left channel and the master volume on your mixer are both up. A good place to set them for now (along with your EQ knobs) is facing up, or in the 12 o'clock position. Even with the speakers currently off or turned down, you should see lights moving on your left channel and master channel showing that music is going through those channels. Adjust the channel gain and master gain so the lights stay in the green and yellow. If either is in the red, turn it down.

4. Turn your speakers up to a comfortable level and listen to the music.

5. Next, load a song on the right deck and bring the fader up on channel 2. Move the crossfader to the right side and listen to that song.

6. Use the channel fader to control the volume of channel 2 and use the crossfader to choose which side you want to hear.

7. Get comfortable touching the jogwheel to play and pause the track with your hand. Also, spin the jogwheel clockwise and counter-clockwise to move around in the song.

8. To use the pitch-bend feature, rotate the sides of the jogwheel clockwise and counter-clockwise. If done correctly, this will speed up or slow down the song while rotating and then return to the original speed when released. It shouldn't stop the music.

9. Load different songs using the scroll wheel or by clicking and dragging different songs onto the virtual decks.

ACTIVITY

Spend 15–30 minutes just listening to different songs. Get comfortable loading different songs onto the virtual decks, using the jogwheel, adjusting the pitch control, using the EQ, adjusting the settings in Serato DJ, and overall getting familiar with your equipment.

TROUBLESHOOTING

If your music is not playing, or it's distorted, use this checklist to troubleshoot:

- If you don't hear anything, make sure the input selector on each channel is set to PC and that the master volume on your controller is up. Also, make sure the Crossfader Assign switch is set to A for the left side and B for right side.

- Make sure all your cables are firmly plugged in between the DJ controller, computer, and speakers.

- Make sure your speakers are turned up.

- Check the On/Off switches for all the equipment and make sure everything is ON.

- Make sure the channel filter or any channel effects are not on.

- Reset Serato DJ or the DJ controller and repeat the steps above.

- If you still can't hear anything, you may have faulty equipment that needs to be repaired.

At this point you should have your DJ gear fully set up, whether you're using turntables (with vinyl or DVS), CDJs (with CDs or DVS), or a DJ controller, with the ability to play music from the left and right sides and hearing it out of your speakers.

Note: *From this point on, all the instructions will be translatable to any type of DJ setup. So, no matter what setup you are using, make sure you've read the manuals for all your gear, adjusted all the settings to your preference, know how to troubleshoot common issues, and in general are comfortable using your equipment. Further, the word "deck" will now be used in place of "turntable," "CDJ," and "jogwheel."*

ADDING HEADPHONES

Headphones are used to cue up the next song that you want to play without interrupting the song that is currently playing. This works because the headphone controls are independent of the main output. So even when you adjust the headphone volume or what's cued up in the headphones, it won't affect the master output.

Headphone controls come in the form of a small crossfader that moves from left to right like a regular crossfader, or "Cue" buttons on each channel that let you select which channel you want to hear in the headphones. The controls include a separate volume knob as well.

You'll have to find a way to get comfortable using headphones and leaving them on your head without them getting in the way of your DJing. Most DJs rest their headphones on their head the entire night with one side on an ear and one side off. This makes it easier to hear what's cued up in the headphones and what's playing out of the speakers at the same time. This also lets you keep your headphones in one place throughout your DJ set—on your head.

Be careful with the headphone volume because, over time, having the volume too loud can result in hearing loss.

PLAYING SONGS FROM THE BEGINNING

Now that you're able to play music out of the left and right decks, let's get started learning how to play music like a DJ. On the left deck, you are going to cue up a song to the very beginning.

With either your needle at the outer edge of the record, a song loaded on the CDJ, or a song loaded on the virtual deck, hit play until you hear the very first sound of the song. Once you do, hit the stop button. If music immediately played when you hit start or you let it play too long, spin the deck counter-clockwise until you reach the first point of silence. Note that if you spin it very slow, the volume will be quiet, which may trick you into thinking that you're at the beginning when you're not. Once you get back to the beginning, be very precise getting to that first initial sound. This may require you to spin the deck back and forth with very small motions. Now do the same on the right deck.

With the crossfader all the way on the left side, hit play on the left deck. Let it play for a minute and slowly move the crossfader to the right side and hit play on the right deck at the same time. You should have heard a smooth fade out of the left song that faded into the right song.

ADDING HEADPHONES

Now, connect your headphones to your gear and cue them for the left deck. With a song playing out of the speakers on the right side, cue up a new song on the left side at the very beginning. Make sure the crossfader is completely on the right side. You don't want to hear the sound of yourself cueing up the left side coming out of the speakers. It should only be heard in the headphones. Once that's done and you're ready, slowly move the crossfader from the right side to the left and hit the left play button at the same time.

Congratulations—you've just performed your first three-song mix. With that simple skill, you could DJ an event right now if you wanted to just casually play songs straight through for the duration.

MARKING THE RECORD (VINYL RECORDS)

One tool vinyl DJs use to easily find the beginning of a record is using a sticker or placing a marking at the very top of the inside record label once they cue it up. This allows you to easily see where the song begins, so you always know how to orient your record while cueing it up.

Using a sticker or marking to show where song begins on vinyl

CUE POINTS (SERATO DJ)

If you're using Serato DJ, you can use cue points to reliably get back to the beginning of a song. Since cue points let you jump to any part of a song, it's helpful to set a cue point at the very beginning of every song you play. In Serato DJ, the cue point section is at the top left of the screen. Simply line up the song where you want the cue point and hit one of the "+" buttons to set it. Then you can press that button to quickly return to that cue point.

Setting Serato DJ cue points

CHAPTER 4: KNOW YOUR RECORDS

 One of my favorite DJs always says, "Know your records!" That means, as a DJ, you should know all the key attributes of every song that you play. Who wrote it? What year was it released? What genre is it? Is it fast or slow? And so on. Think of songs as being like Lego sculptures. You may have one large final sculpture, but it's comprised of many smaller and essential components, and you need to know and understand all of those if you want to fit them all together to build that final masterpiece.

SONG ATTRIBUTES (0:00–8:10)

Knowing what each song that you play is made of—those "small Lego pieces"— will make you a better DJ because that understanding of all the ways they could connect with each other will help you put together more creative and unique sets of music.

Here are the main general attributes of a song:

- **Artist:** Who wrote the song? Who are other similar artists?

- **Year:** In what year, decade, or musical era did this come out? Is it new, kind of new, a throwback, old school, really old?

- **Genre:** What style of music is it? Rap, pop, R&B, soul, reggae, other?

- **Topic:** What is the artist talking about in the song?

- **Energy Level:** On a scale of 1–10, how chill or hype is the song?

- **Song Title:** This may sound simple, but certain songs with similar titles sometimes fit well.

- **Mood:** How does the song make you feel? Happy, sad, angry, neutral?

Let's try a quick song attribute exercise:

1. List five songs you like that were released between 2000–2009.

Artist _____ Song Title _____ Year _____

Artist _____ Song Title _____ Year _____

Artist _____ Song Title _____ Year _____

Artist _____ Song Title _____ Year _____

Artist _____ Song Title _____ Year _____

2. List five songs of any genre that you consider high energy.

Artist _____ Song Title _____ Energy Level _____

Artist _____ Song Title _____ Energy Level _____

Artist _____ Song Title _____ Energy Level _____

Artist _____ Song Title _____ Energy Level _____

Artist _____ Song Title _____ Energy Level _____

3. List five songs that talk about love.

Artist _____ Song Title_____

Artist _____ Song Title_____

Artist _____ Song Title_____

Artist _____ Song Title_____

Artist _____ Song Title_____

SONG INSTRUMENTATION

OK, now that you're thinking like a DJ, let's look at the instrumentation of songs. This is just asking the question, "What do the instruments and vocals sound like in the song?"

- **Drums**: How hard or soft are the drums in the song? Are they live drums or pre-programmed drums? Does the song even have drums?

- **Instruments:** What instruments do you hear in the song? Piano, guitar, violins, trumpets, synths, a sample from an older song?

- **Melody:** Does the song have a *hook*—a specific pattern of musical notes that you remember? (A great example of this are the horns at the beginning of Pete Rock and C.L. Smooth's classic hip-hop song "They Reminisce Over You.")

- **Vocals:** What does the singer or rapper sound like on the song? Is their voice smooth or rugged? Powerful or tame?

INSTRUMENTATION EXERCISE

1. List five songs with a prominent horn section (e.g., J Balvin's "Mi Gente").

Artist _____ Song Title_____

Artist _____ Song Title_____

Artist _____ Song Title_____

Artist _____ Song Title_____

Artist _____ Song Title_____

2. List five singers with strong, powerful voices like Adele.

Artist _____

Artist _____

Artist _____

Artist _____

Artist _____

Great! Now you're thinking even more like a DJ, but to become a great one, you have to go even further to deepen your understanding of music.

TEMPO AND BPM ▶ (8:11–14:30)

The *tempo* of a song is just the speed of the beats, and that is commonly measured in beats per minute, or BPM. The "beat" is determined by the time signature of the song. For example, a song with a 4/4 time signature has four quarter-note beats per measure, so a song with a tempo of 120 BPM in 4/4 time equates to 120 quarter notes in one minute. **For a DJ, the BPM indicates how many times you nod your head or tap your feet to a song in one minute.**

Understanding the BPM is extremely important as a DJ because this will be the main factor in determining whether two songs will be able to mix well together or not. If two songs are at the same BPM, or tempo, and are playing in sync with each other, when you transition between the two, it will sound smooth. And as a DJ, you want those seamless transitions between every song.

FINDING THE BPM OF A SONG

Serato DJ and all other DJ software will analyze your songs and give you detailed information about it with just the press of a button. In Serato DJ, you can load a song onto a virtual deck or hit the "Analyze Files" button to do so.

Use the Analyze Files button to find BPM

It will determine the BPM, song key, bitrate, length, size, sample rate, and show all of the relevant song data like the song name, artist, album name, and where the file is located on your computer. This is a great feature but it's not 100% accurate, so you'll need to know how to figure this out on your own too.

FINDING THE BPM ACTIVITY

To find a song's BPM without using software, you will need a stopwatch—either an actual watch or the stopwatch app on your smart phone. Play a song for which you want to find the BPM and start to nod your head or tap your foot to the beat. Once you've found the rhythm and are comfortable with it, hit start on the stopwatch and begin to count the number of head nods or foot taps in 60 seconds. Write in your answer below. Do this for three songs in your music library.

Artist _____ Song Title _____ BPM _____

Artist _____ Song Title _____ BPM _____

Artist _____ Song Title _____ BPM _____

As a reference, the tempo for "Check the Rhime" by A Tribe Called Quest is 96 BPM. Try to count it yourself and see if you are correct. Your answer could very possibly be anywhere between 92–100 and that's OK. You aren't a robot, you're a human! As a DJ, you'll use the BPM as a reference point to connect one song to another.

For example, let's say you want to connect "Check the Rhime" to "Hypnotize" by Notorious B.I.G., which has a tempo of 94 BPM. Since the BPMs of both songs don't match up perfectly, you'll need to use the pitch control to either speed up "Hypnotize" or slow down "Check the Rhime" before you try to blend them together—playing one after the other. And since their tempos are so close, you won't have to adjust either one very much.

COUNTING BARS ▶ (14:31–end)

To put it simply, a "bar," in DJ terms, comprises four quarter notes, or four beats. Fortunately, almost all of the music you'll DJ with (especially hip-hop, rock, and pop) is in the 4/4 time signature, so you almost never have to be concerned with bars that don't follow this structure. Keeping this in mind, every time you nod your head to a song four times, you just counted a bar. Bar counts help you understand the structure of your music and let you know when to bring in the next song.

Let's look at Lil Jon's "Snap Yo Fingers" as an example. If you have the song in your music library, cue it up. If not, you can play it on YouTube. As soon as the song starts, nod your head and count the beats, starting at "1." But unlike counting the BPM, when you continue to count higher, you'll just do a four-count for each bar throughout the song, like this:

1-2-3-4   **1**-2-3-4   **1**-2-3-4   **1**-2-3-4

For now, just get used to saying the four-count out loud and staying on beat.

FINDING THE "ONE"

It's important to make sure that when you start your bar count, you "find the one," or the *downbeat*. Usually, when the song begins, or when the drums come in, or when the "drop" happens in EDM music, that's the "one." For example, the "one" in DJ Snake and Lil Jon's "Turn Down for What" is at the drop, and it's the cue for you to start the bar count.

COUNTING BARS OF A SECTION

You can use your knowledge of bars to determine how long certain sections of songs are—not "long" in the sense of minutes and seconds, but rather how many bars each section comprises. When counting the number of bars of a section, you perform the same four-count, but replace the "1" with the number of the bar you're on, like this:

1-2-3-4   **2**-2-3-4   **3**-2-3-4   **4**-2-3-4

That was four bars. Now, cue up "Snap Yo Fingers" again and count how many bars are in the intro, which spans from the very beginning of the song right up to the chorus where Lil Jon says, "Snap yo fingers, do yo step" (00:00–00:23 seconds). If you did it correctly, you should have counted eight bars, which would have ended with you counting "**8**-2-3-4." If you didn't get that, try it again until you do.

Let's look at the bar counts for each section for the rest of the song:

Song section:	Intro	Chorus	Verse 1	Chorus	Verse 2	Chorus	Verse 3	Chorus	Outro
Bar count:	8 bars	8 bars	12 bars	8 bars	16 bars	8 bars	16 bars	8 bars	8 bars
Time:	00:00–00:23	00:23–00:47	00:47–01:22	01:22–01:45	01:45–02:32	02:32–02:56	02:56–03:42	03:42–04:06	04:06–04:29

"Snap Yo Fingers" bar count

Notice how the chorus, intro, and outro are all eight bars, and the verses are either 12 or 16. Most songs will follow this pattern where the chorus, intro, outro, and bridge will be four or eight bars, and the verses will be 8, 12, or 16. Often times, the intros and outros of songs don't include any vocalists rapping or singing, so those are the best moments in which to transition to a new song.

COUNT THE BARS ACTIVITY

Pick out a song in your music library and count the bars of each section. Label each section and note the bar count. If you're having trouble picking a song, try Ol' Dirty Bastard's "Got Your Money."

Artist: _____ Song Title: _____

Section: _____ Bar Length: _____

Section: _____ Bar Length: _____

Section: _____ Bar Length: _____

Section: _____ Bar Length: _____

Section: _____ Bar Length: _____

Section: _____ Bar Length: _____

Section: _____ Bar Length: _____

Section: _____ Bar Length: _____

Section: _____ Bar Length: _____

Section: _____ Bar Length: _____

As you progress, you will take all of this information about the songs you play to build your sets and determine your style of DJing. At first, you might group songs based on genre or the decade it was released. But you can go deeper and group them together by BPM, genre, and decade. For example, you could create a playlist in Serato DJ of 1990s hip-hop songs all around 100 BPM or new pop songs around 120 BPM.

Then, based on the energy level and bar count of each, you can figure out what order you want to play them in. After that, if you know the bar count of each of those songs, you'll know when you should begin and end your transition for each song. Take *everything* you know about each song into account when you make a transition so that each one is unique.

Eventually, you'll find that instead of saying, "At the 1:30 mark of the song..." you'll say things like:

- "At the second chorus..."

- "After the third verse..."

- "At the beginning of the breakdown that occurs near the end..."

- "I'll start my transition at the second chorus of this song and blend it with the intro of the song I have cued up—since both sections are eight bars—and I'll end the transition at the end of those eight bars."

This is how you think like a DJ.

CHAPTER 5: SCRATCHING 101

 To put it simply, *scratching* is the act of rotating the deck forward and backward to create percussive or rhythmic sounds. Some of the first hip-hop songs to feature scratching are Grandmaster Flash's "The Adventures of Grandmaster Flash on the Wheels of Steel," Malcolm McLaren and the World's Famous Supreme Team's "Buffalo Gals," and Herbie Hancock's Grammy Award-winning single "Rockit."

Scratching adds another dimension to your DJing. It also helps with timing and catching the rhythm of a song. There are literally hundreds of different scratches to learn, but in this section we will focus on just a few to get you started. And remember, scratching is like seasoning your food—it's best when used sparingly and purposefully.

Note: You can use the crossfader to add more style and rhythm to your scratches. Make sure the Crossfader Curve on your mixer is set to "Fast" when scratching.

BABY SCRATCH ▶ (0:00–9:58)

The first scratch everyone learns is the *baby scratch*. This is literally just rotating the deck forward and backward to the beat of a song.

With your DJ gear on and ready to go, cue up the very beginning of a song on either deck. If you're using turntables, take note of the orientation of the record sticker; if you're using jogwheels, take note of which angle the light is facing. This will be your visual cue for where to bring the song back to, since that is the start point of your scratch sound. In the images below, the scratch sound starts with the white Serato label on the record facing up.

Also, whether you're using the left or right deck, place your hand toward the outer edge of the middle left side of the deck, around 9 o'clock.

Left deck with left hand on left side of record   *Right deck with right hand on left side of record*

With your hand on the deck, hit Play but don't let the deck move. Now, rotate the deck forward (clockwise) and then back (counter-clockwise) to the original starting point. Start with very small rotations and work your way up to larger movements. Do slow movements and fast movements. Just make sure that with every scratch, on the way back, you bring the song back to the original starting point. Now do the same with the other deck. You'll need to get comfortable scratching with both hands. Spend about 5–10 minutes with each hand scratching the beginning of the song.

Baby Scratch Motion

| 1. Starting position | 2. Forward movement | 3. Ending position |

Note: For vinyl users, make sure you're light-handed when using the records. Applying too much pressure when scratching can cause the needle to jump out of the groove and move to a different part of the song.

Make sure the scratch sounds punchy—not mushy. If your scratch sounds mushy, you're probably not rotating the song back to its original starting point. Rotate the song back a little bit more until right before the sound starts and try again. For example, if you're scratching a kick-drum sound, it should sound like knocking on a door, not rubbing on a door. It will sound almost like "duff-a-duff-a" when performed correctly.

Now, let the song play and find an interesting part you want to scratch, such as a weird vocal section, instrument solo, or a cool drum pattern. Cue up the record to the beginning of that specific sound and scratch that. Different parts of a song will sound different when you scratch them. Parts that stand out the most are kick drums, snare drums, and vocals. For example, at the beginning of "Paul Revere" by the Beastie Boys, they say "Nooooow" really loud and high pitched. Scratching that part can be extremely fun.

There are vinyl records or MP3s you can purchase that only have sounds and phrases for scratching. These are called *scratch records* or *scratch sentences*. Purchase a few to use for practice.

SCRATCH TO THE BEAT

As mentioned, when you scratch, you always want it to have a purpose—so let's give it one. On the right deck, play a song you're familiar with. On the left, cue up a sound you'd like to scratch. Now, nod your head to the beat of the song playing on the right, and with every head nod, baby scratch the left deck forward then backward.

If it's too fast to stay on beat, use the pitch control to slow down the song on the right. Or if it's too slow and feels too easy, use the pitch control to speed it up or pick a different song that's faster. Do this for at least five minutes.

Now pick a different song you'd like to scratch to—something you may not be as familiar with—and play it on the left deck. Cue up a different sound you'd like to scratch on the right side and repeat the exercise. Make sure that with every movement you are focusing on being precise and bringing the scratch sound back to its original starting point.

Practice for at least 15 minutes with each hand.

FORWARD OR "STAB" SCRATCH ▶️ (9:59–14:06)

The forward scratch, or *stab*, has the same motion as the baby scratch, but as the name says, you're only going to hear the forward sound, not the pull back. To perform this, one hand will need to be on the deck (record hand), and the other will be on the crossfader (fader hand).

Like you did with the baby scratch, find a sound that you'd like to scratch on the left deck. Once you have that sound cued up, make sure the crossfader is in the middle. The image below is the starting position.

Stab scratch starting position

1. Move left deck forward to hear the forward motion of the scratch and leave the crossfader in the middle.

Stab scratch, forward motion complete

2. Close the crossfader (move the crossfader all the way to the right).

Stab scratch with crossfader pushed right

3. Spin the record back to the beginning of the sound, with the crossfader still closed (all the way to the right).

Stab scratch, record hand back to start position

4. Move the crossfader back to the middle.

Stab scratch, crossfader back to start position

5. Repeat.

If done correctly, you'll only hear the forward motion of the scratch. Similar to the baby scratch, try this using a kick-drum sound or a long vocal sample like someone singing a sustained note. And as you progress, switch hands and use your right hand as your scratch hand on the right deck, and your left hand as the fader hand on the crossfader.

SCRATCH TO THE BEAT

On the right deck, play a song you're familiar with. On the left, cue up a sound you'd like to forward scratch. Now, nod your head to the beat of the song playing on the right and perform the forward scratch on beat with that song. This is tougher than the baby scratch, so start slowly.

If it's too fast to stay on beat, use the pitch control to slow down the song on the right. Likewise, if it's too slow and feels too easy, use the pitch control to speed it up or pick a different song that's even faster. Do this for at least five minutes.

Now pick a different song you'd like to scratch to—something you may not be as familiar with—and play it on the left deck. Cue up a different sound you'd like to scratch on the right side and repeat the exercise. Note that closing the crossfader will now mean moving the crossfader all the way to the left. Make sure that with every scratch you are focusing on being precise, bringing your scratch sound back to its original starting point, and closing the fader.

Practice for at least 15 minutes with each hand.

TRANSFORM SCRATCH ▶ (14:07–20:25)

The *transform scratch* allows you to "chop up" your scratch sample into multiple pieces. Essentially, you're opening and closing the crossfader very quickly so it sounds like the volume is going in and out just as quickly. To do this, you'll need to use your thumb as a spring on the crossfader to keep pushing it closed, while you use your middle or pointer finger to tap it open. This scratch works best with a longer sample, so avoid kick-drum sounds for this. Try using a long vocal sample like an "Ahhhhhhh" or "Heeeeeey."

Start with your scratch sample cued up on your record hand (left side for this example) and your right hand on the fader with the fader closed. In addition, your right thumb needs to be pushed up against the fader to keep it closed (all the way to the right), as seen in the photo. You'll be applying that pressure with your thumb throughout this entire exercise. This is the starting position of the transform scratch.

Starting position for transform scratch

1. Slowly move the left deck clockwise, but with a longer motion than normal. Make sure you're playing the entire sample.

2. At the same time, while you're moving the deck clockwise, tap the crossfader twice with your right middle or pointer finger to open it. Your right thumb should still be applying pressure to the crossfader so it will close quickly. If done correctly, you should have heard two short snippets of your scratch sample.

Record hand and fader hand positions for transform scratch

3. As you pull the record back, tap the crossfader twice with your right middle or pointer finger to open it.

4. You should end with the crossfader closed, with your thumb still applying pressure to it.

In total, you should have heard four distinct sounds—two forward and two backward—to complete your transform scratch. You can tap the crossfader as many or as few times as you want going forward or backward, so try different combinations. Try two taps forward and one tap backward, or three taps forward and one tap backward. It will take time to get used to performing two different motions with each hand, but eventually you'll get to the point where your record hand is completely smooth going forward and backward, and your fader hand is relaxed yet precise and on time.

SCRATCH TO THE BEAT

On the right deck, play a song you're familiar with. On the left, cue up a sound you'd like to transform scratch. Nod your head to the beat of the song playing on the right and perform the transform scratch on beat with that song. This is tougher than both the baby scratch and the forward scratch, so start slowly.

If it's too fast to stay on beat, use the pitch control to slow down the song on the right. Likewise, if it's too slow and feels too easy, use the pitch control to speed it up or pick a different song that's faster. Do this for at least five minutes.

Next, switch hands and try to transform scratch on the right side, with your right hand as the record hand and your left as the fader hand. Note that closing the crossfader will now mean moving the crossfader all the way to the left. Make sure that with every scratch you are focusing on being precise, bringing your scratch sound back to its original starting point, and using your thumb to close the fader after each tap.

Practice for at least 15 minutes with each hand, changing how many taps you perform going forward and backward.

CHIRP SCRATCH ▶ (20:26–26:35)

The last beginner scratch is the *chirp scratch*. The purpose of this technique is to make your sample sound sharper when you're scratching it. With this scratch, you're essentially cutting off the tail ends of the forward and backward motion of the sound, so the sound going forward and backward will be short bursts. This scratch works best with shorter samples like a kick-drum sound or a short vocal sample.

1. Start with the fader in the middle and your scratch sample cued up on the left turntable.

Chirp scratch starting position

2. Now, at the exact same time, move the record forward and close the fader by pushing it all the way to the right. You should have heard just a snippet of the sound moving forward before the crossfader cut it off.

Chirp scratch, forward motion complete

3. Now, at the exact same time, spin the record back to the beginning of the scratch sound and move the crossfader back to the middle. Again, you should have heard a snippet of the record moving backward.

The most important thing with this scratch is precision. Make sure your record movements are controlled and that every time you spin it back, you bring it back to the exact beginning of the sample, or else it won't sound good. Your hands will be going out together and in together. Think "elbows out, elbows in" as you begin to practice this scratch.

SCRATCH TO THE BEAT

On the right deck, play a song you're familiar with. On the left, cue up a sound you'd like to chirp scratch. Nod your head to the beat of the song playing on the right and perform the chirp scratch on beat with that song. The chirp scratch should be easier than the transform scratch as long as you stay precise.

If it's too fast to stay on beat, use the pitch control to slow down the song on the right. Likewise, if it's too slow and feels too easy, use the pitch control to speed it up or pick a different song that's even faster. Do this for at least five minutes.

Next, switch hands and chirp scratch on the right side, with your right hand as the record hand and your left as the fader hand. Note that closing the crossfader will now mean moving the crossfader all the way to the left. Make sure that with every scratch you are focusing on being precise and bringing your scratch sound back to its original starting point.

Practice for at least 15 minutes with each hand using songs of various speeds.

FORWARD ("STAB") SCRATCH REVISITED ▶ (26:36–29:51)

Now that you've learned how to perform transform and chirp scratches, you can use those techniques to help you perform the forward (or stab) scratch more easily. You will use your thumb like a spring as in the transform scratch, and you'll need the precision and timing of the chirp scratch.

Start with your scratch sample cued up on your record hand (left side for this example) and your right hand on the crossfader with the crossfader closed. In addition, your right thumb needs to be pushed up against the crossfader to keep it closed (all the way to the right), as seen in the photo. You'll be applying that pressure with your thumb throughout this entire exercise. To review, this is the starting position of the stab scratch.

Starting position for stab scratch

1. Perform a full baby scratch (forward and backward) with your scratch hand and at the same time tap the crossfader once with your right middle or index finger to open it. Your right thumb should still be applying pressure to the crossfader so it will close quickly.

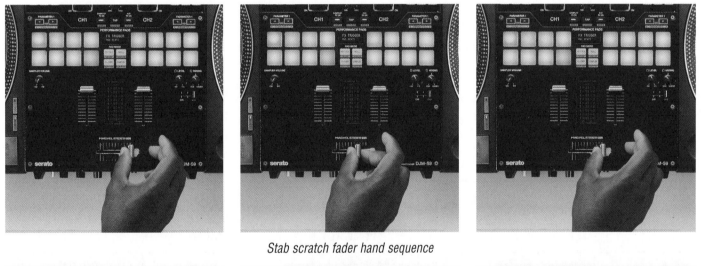

Stab scratch fader hand sequence

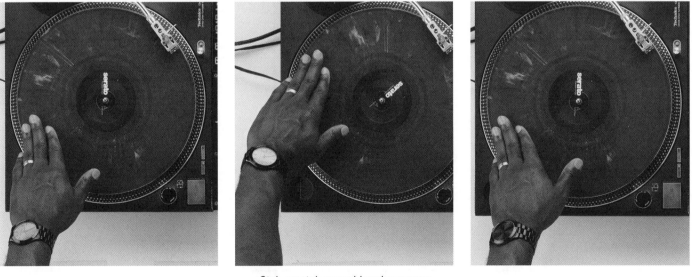

Stab scratch record hand sequence

2. Your thumb should close the crossfader quickly enough so that you only hear the forward motion of the scratch. This scratch seems easy, but it takes time to master. Your timing has to be extremely precise between your scratch hand and your fader hand, so give yourself time to learn this.

SCRATCH TO THE BEAT

On the right deck, play a song you're familiar with. On the left, cue up a sound you'd like to use for this new way of performing a stab scratch. Nod your head to the beat of the song playing on the right and perform the stab scratch on beat with that song. Perform this scratch at a tempo that's comfortable for you, and as you progress, speed up the song using the pitch control or find a faster song if necessary.

Now pick a different song you'd like to scratch to—something you may not be as familiar with—and play it on the left deck. Cue up a different sound you'd like to scratch on the right side and repeat the exercise. Note that closing the crossfader will now mean moving the crossfader all the way to the left. Make sure that with every scratch you are focusing on being precise, bringing your scratch sound back to its original starting point, and closing the crossfader quickly with your thumb acting as a spring.

Practice for at least 15 minutes with each hand.

SCRATCHING EXERCISES ▶️ (29:52–end)

You just learned four scratches: baby, forward (stab), transform, and chirp. You'll need to practice each of these scratches often to truly get them down. The best way to do that is by performing the scratch at a specific BPM, and as it becomes easier at that tempo, speed up the song or find a faster track to scratch to. You'll also need to practice with both hands going forward then backward, and backward then forward. Think about it like lifting weights at the gym. You start at a weight with which you're comfortable and then move up as you get stronger.

Use the chart below to track the BPM at which you can perform each scratch on beat comfortably for eight bars. Keep practicing the specific scratch, and as you get faster, update the chart to track your progress. As you learn more scratches, fill in the rows at the bottom of the table with those.

For example, with the baby scratch row, write in how fast you can perform a baby scratch for eight bars going forward to backward with your left hand. In the second column, write in how fast you perform the baby scratch starting at the end of the scratch sample going backward to forward with your left hand. In the last two columns, switch to your right hand and do the same.

Scratch	Left Hand (Forward-Backward)	Left Hand (Backward-Forward)	Right Hand (Forward-Backward)	Right Hand (Backward-Forward)
Baby				
Forward (Stab)				
Transform (1 forward – 1 backward)				
Transform (2 forward – 2 backward)				
Chirp				

Note: If you reach tempos faster than 130–140 BPM, go back down to 65–70 BPM and do the scratches in double time. For example, instead of one baby scratch every beat, you'll perform two baby scratches every beat.

CHAPTER 6: TRANSITIONS BETWEEN SONGS

 As a DJ, transitioning between songs is one of the most important parts of the job. When it's done right, it sounds like the two songs you mixed were glued together perfectly; but when it's off, it sounds like shoes in a dryer. In other words, when a DJ makes a smooth transition, everyone notices, and when a DJ makes a bad transition, everyone *really* notices. So it's important to learn different ways to transition and use what makes sense for each song you play.

In this section, we'll focus on three of the most common ways to transition between songs: fading, slamming, and blending.

FADING (0:00–3:32)

The good news is you essentially already know how to perform the fading technique. You practiced it in the headphone section. *Fading* is the simple act of moving the crossfader from one side to the other to play the next song. So, if you have a song playing on the left side, cue up a song at the beginning on the right side in the headphones. Then, as the song on the left ends (fades out), hit play on the right side and slowly move the crossfader from left to right. The overall volume of the music shouldn't drop very much, and if you picked two similar songs, the songs won't clash.

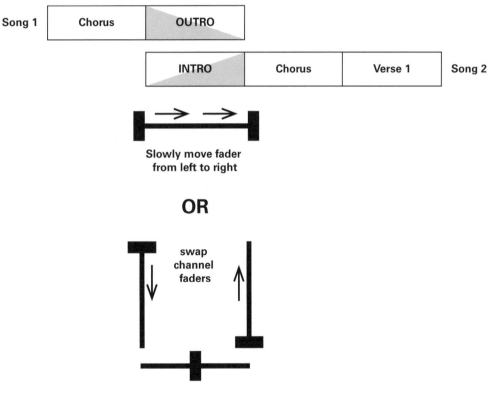

Fade-in transition flow chart

This technique is great for when you're DJing in a more relaxed environment, such as a backyard BBQ or a picnic. In this situation, your main focus should be song selection, making sure you pick the right songs to play at the right time.

Tip: Sometimes songs have a breakdown or a drop in the energy in the middle of the song, so you can use that part to fade in the next song without having to wait all the way until the end.

FADE-IN ACTIVITY

Pick two songs in your music library that fade out at the end and load them onto your decks. Cue both of them up to the very beginning and play the left deck. As that song begins to fade out, hit play on the right deck while moving the crossfader over to the right side. This should be very simple.

Next, while the right song is playing, cue up the left song back to the beginning using your headphones. Do it quickly so that it's ready before the song on the right is over. As the song on the right fades out, play the song on the left deck from the beginning and move the crossfader back to the left side.

Repeat this back-and-forth process as many times as you need to feel comfortable switching between songs. And as you get better and quicker, switch in different songs and see if you can string together at least five different songs.

SLAMMING ▶ (3:33–8:38)

The next transition technique is called *slamming in* the next song, *aka* "slip-cueing." The goal with this type of transition is to switch songs instantaneously, while keeping the two songs on beat or on time. That is, if you're dancing or nodding your head to the first song, when you slam in the next, you'll be able to keep nodding your head or dancing without any change in rhythm.

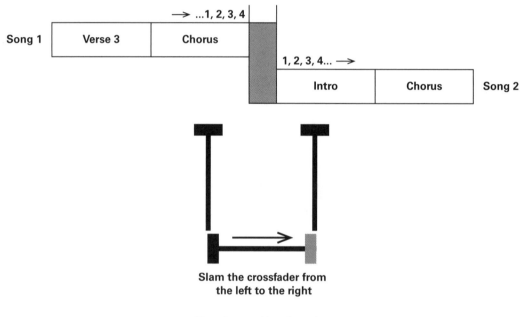

Slam-in transition flow chart

Let's take a step-by-step look at slamming:

1. Play a song on the left deck, making sure the crossfader is all the way to the left so only the left deck can be heard out of the speakers.

2. In the headphones, cue up a song at the beginning on the right deck that has a similar BPM. It doesn't have to be exact, but it should be within a ±5 BPM range.

3. On that right deck (in the headphones), find the first downbeat (the "one") of the song.

4. Place your hand on the right deck and hit play but don't let go. Just hold the song right there at that first downbeat.

5. Count the bar count of the song on the left (1-2-3-4, 1-2-3-4, etc.), and at the same time perform a full baby scratch (forward and backward motion) on the right deck at each beat.

6. You should hear yourself baby scratching in the headphones to the beat of the left deck. Make sure the baby scratch sounds punchy and not mushy.

7. Keep doing this for about six to eight bars, and when you're ready, let go of the record on the right deck on the "one" and move the crossfader as quick as you can from left to right at the same time.

8. If done correctly, there shouldn't be a break in the music and the song on the right should come in on time.

This type of transition is great when there's no breakdown in the song you're playing, or if it has a very abrupt end and you want to keep the crowd moving and their energy level up. It may take a while to get the timing down, but practice this with multiple songs and different speeds.

SLAMMING IN ACTIVITY

Pick five songs in your music library that are very close in BPM and use the slamming-in technique to transition between them. Make sure to use the headphones to find the "one" at the beginning of each song before you bring it in. Slam in as many songs as you need to feel comfortable switching between songs. As you improve and are able to make faster transitions, add in more songs or repeat using the five songs you originally selected.

BLENDING RECORDS ▶ (8:39–18:22)

Blending records is the process of playing two songs on top of each other that are at the same BPM and in sync, while seamlessly transitioning between the two. If songs aren't the same BPM, you'll need to use the pitch control to adjust the speeds of one or both songs until they match. Blending records is important so your crowd can continue to dance without any interruption or break in the music. This is one of the most essential skills that a DJ should have, and it adds an unmatched layer of style and creativity to your DJing.

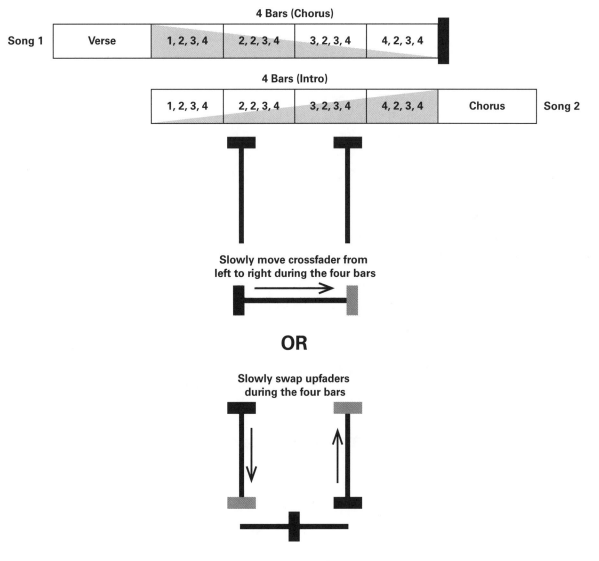

Blending transition flow chart

An easy way to picture how blending works is imagining two cars driving on the freeway next to each other at the same speed. During the transition between songs, your goal is to keep the two songs lined up right next to each other, just like those two cars. If the song you have cued up is too slow, even if you started them at the same time, they will slowly drift apart from each other. So you'll need to speed it up to keep them perfectly in sync.

TOO SLOW

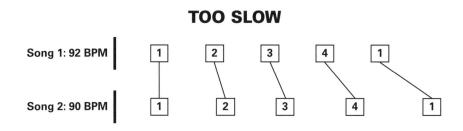

If song 2 tempo is too slow, it will lag behind song 1

Conversely, if it's too fast, you'll need to slow it down.

TOO FAST

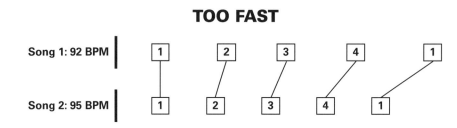

If song 2 tempo is too fast, it will speed ahead of song 1

Alternatively, if both songs are the same BPM, but the beats aren't perfectly synchronized, you'll need to push or pull one song to get it synched up. Think of songs that aren't synched as two cars traveling the same speed, but one car being a few feet behind the other. It will need to speed up for a short time, but once caught up, it can return to the original speed.

SAME TEMPO – NOT IN SYNC (Released too late)

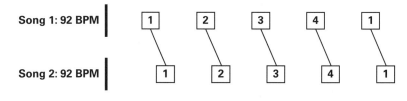

Tempos match, but the downbeats weren't synchronized

It takes time to master this technique so don't feel discouraged if it seems difficult at first. Good blending requires the ability to listen to two songs at once, while trying to differentiate between them, which isn't easy. It takes years to completely master, but once you do you'll be able to mix all different types of music together with ease.

SAME TEMPO – IN-SYNC

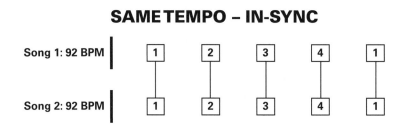

Properly synchronized songs

BLENDING WITH IDENTICAL RECORDS

Timing is the most important element when it comes to blending records. *Timing*, in this case, is the skill of dropping the song that's cued up on beat with the song playing, so that the songs end up perfectly in sync with each other. The first exercise to help get your timing correct is blending the same song with itself. If the songs aren't synched with each other, you'll immediately hear it and have to try again. When you do it right, they'll stay synched until the song ends.

1. Put a song you're familiar with on both the left and right deck. Use a song with drums throughout the entire track, including at the beginning.

2. Listen to the song and find the "one."

3. Set both the left and right pitch controls to zero and play the left song. Let the track play for a bit to catch the rhythm of the song. Literally, just nod your head or tap your foot to it and find the groove.

4. In the headphones, cue up the right side to the first downbeat ("one") and baby scratch that downbeat to the tempo of the song on the left side. While scratching, count "1-2-3-4" to the bar count of the left side.

5. After you've done that a few times and are feeling ready, perform a "1-2-3-4-go" baby scratch and release the record on the "go." Remember, you are dropping it on the "one," not the "four."

6. Now listen to both the left side (which is coming out of the speakers) and the right side (which is coming out of the headphones) at the same time to determine if both songs are in sync with each other.

7. **Check your mix by pushing and pulling**

   a. If you released it *too late*, the song will be behind, so you'll need to lightly push the platter forward with your finger until the song catches up. Then use the crossfader to slowly fade from the left side to the right. If you're using CDJs or a DJ controller with jogwheels, instead of pushing the platter forward with your finger, you'll need to rotate the pitch-bend wheel on the side of the jogwheel clockwise until the song catches up.

   b. If you released it *too early*, it's ahead, so you'll need to lightly press the platter with your finger to slow the record down until it matches. Then use the crossfader to slowly fade from the left side to the right. If you're using CDJs or a DJ controller with jogwheels, instead of lightly pressing the platter with your finger, you'll need to rotate the pitch-bend wheel on the side of the jogwheel counter-clockwise until the song matches up.

   c. If you released the record *on time*, the songs should be in sync with each other and you can use the crossfader to slowly fade from the left side to the right.

Congratulations! You just performed your first successful blend.

IS IT STILL OFF?

If the transition still doesn't sound in sync, or if you were unable to determine if you released it too late or too early, try it again by repeating the steps of the exercise until you get it right. You'll know when you've done it right because both songs will sound like they're playing at the exact same time.

BLENDING WITH IDENTICAL RECORDS ACTIVITY

With the song on the right playing out of the speakers, cue up the initial downbeat on the left side in the headphones and try to bring it in on beat. Practice this technique over and over, going from one side to the other using identical songs, and your timing will improve. As you progress, try blending other pairs of the same song from different styles, genres, and BPM to get comfortable working with all types of music.

BLENDING DIFFERENT SONGS AT THE SAME TEMPO

Your next goal is to blend two *different* songs that have the same BPM. Since both songs are the same speed but have different sounds, this will help you learn to differentiate two separate songs in your head at once.

To start, find two songs in your music library that have the same BPM. Follow the same steps from the previous section, but this time you'll have to identify the first downbeat in each song separately. Once you've done that, you can begin practicing your blending transition technique. It's helpful to imagine you're DJing a party where the crowd wants to hear the same two songs over and over all night.

Practice this with other songs at faster or slower tempos, as well as with songs from different genres. For example, try to mix a hip-hop song with a reggae song that both have the same BPM, or pick two house songs that sound completely different but are at the same tempo.

BLENDING SONGS WITH DIFFERENT BPM ▶ (18:23–25:33)

Blending songs at different BPM is tough because you'll need to listen to two songs at the same time (one out of the speakers and one through your headphones) and determine which one is slower or faster. Once you've determined that, you'll use the pitch control to adjust the speed of one to match the other.

Note: The pitch controls on standard turntables increase or decrease the pitch by 8%. CDJs and DJ controllers often can go to ±50%, but it's best to stay within the 8% range so your songs don't sound too far off from their original speeds.

1. For your first try, pick two songs that have a difference of only 2–5 BPM.

2. Play the faster song on the left deck and cue up the slower song in your headphones at the first downbeat on the right deck.

3. Perform the "1-2-3-4-go" baby scratch on the right deck and release the record.

4. "Test the blend" by listening to both songs at the same time. The left song will be playing out of the speakers and the right song will be playing in your headphones.

5. If your timing was correct, you'll notice the two songs sounded on beat and in sync at first, but then slowly got more off-beat until you couldn't tell the difference anymore as to which song was faster or slower.

6. Since you already know the right song is too slow, increase the pitch of the right song by 2% (or two notches on your pitch control), cue the right song at the beginning downbeat, and test the blend again.

   a. If the right song still sounds too slow, increase the pitch and test the blend again.

   b. If it sounds like it's now too fast, decrease the pitch a little and test the blend again.

   c. If it sounds like it stayed on beat for at least 5–8 seconds, then you've matched the BPM close enough for this exercise.

7. Once you're confident that you've matched the BPM, cue the right song back to the first downbeat one more time, perform the "1-2-3-4-go" baby scratch on the right song, and release the record. Slowly move the crossfader from the left to right, but let them play on top of each other for a few seconds so you can hear the blend for yourself.

Next, try to blend a different song with a song you know is too fast and follow the previous steps.

Blending is a difficult skill to learn, let alone master, so be patient during this process. Listening to two different songs at once and separating them in your brain is a tough skill in itself. Over time, your goal will be to blend records without knowing the BPM at first and to do it completely by ear. In other words, when you cue up a record and test the blend in the headphones, you'll be able to determine if it's too fast or too slow and make the necessary adjustments to the pitch.

▶ (25:34–28:16)

- The snare (or, the clap) will be the most noticeable sound in your headphones, so try to pay attention to the cued-up song's snare to see if it's coming in too fast or too slow.

- Remember, the songs could be at the same speed but not in sync with each other, so get used to pushing or pulling the song with your hand using the platter or pitch-bend wheel. This is especially important when DJing with live songs because the BPM will change throughout the song.

- Songs playing at different BPM can fall in and out of sync with each other, giving the impression that, for the moment, they are at the same speed. Make sure you let the blend ride for a long enough time to be sure this is not the case.

- You only need a few seconds to blend one song into the next, so if the beats don't match forever, that's OK.

- If you're DJing on a loud system, use the bass vibrations as a way to feel the beat.

- Try mixing different genres of music together and keeping them on beat. For example, reggae music has a different drum pattern than old-school hip-hop, so keeping them on beat and blending them together is good practice.

- An advanced technique is playing an *a capella* version of a song (vocals alone with no instruments) over an instrumental version of a song and keeping the a capella on beat and in sync with the instrumental. Use this method with a song you're familiar with to perfect your beat-matching skills.

WHEN TO TRANSITION

Knowing when and how to transition to the next song is based on the structure and sound of the song you're playing. For example, if you know the chorus of the song you're playing is eight bars and the intro of the song you have cued up is also eight bars (and they are both at the same tempo), you can blend those two sections together to make for a smooth transition.

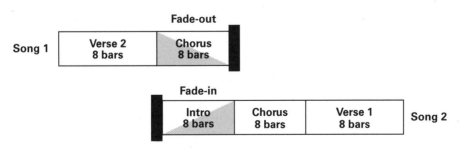

"When to transition" flowchart

Let's revisit "Snap Yo Fingers" by Lil Jon for an exercise. From the earlier chapter, you know that each chorus of that song is eight bars. So if you can find another song at the same tempo that has an eight-bar intro, such as "The Rain" by Missy Elliott, you can blend these two sections together.

Since these are both popular throwback hip-hop songs, they will fit together well simply because of their genre. The tempo of "Snap Yo Fingers" is 82 BPM and "The Rain" is 80 BPM, so you'll either have to speed up "The Rain" or slow down "Snap Yo Fingers." If you have these two songs in your library or can purchase them, try to match their BPM.

From the first downbeat of "The Rain" to when the first verse starts is eight bars. Keeping that in mind, let "Snap Yo Fingers" play from the beginning. During its intro, as it nears the first chorus, start performing a baby scratch on the first downbeat of "The Rain," making sure you're on beat and in sync with "Snap Yo Fingers." Put the crossfader in the middle so you can hear your scratching out of the speakers. As soon as the chorus of "Snap Yo Fingers" starts, let go of the deck playing "The Rain" on the "one." If executed correctly, they should be playing in sync with each other. Next, as the chorus of "Snap Yo Fingers" ends, move the crossfader completely over to the side on which "The Rain" is playing. At this point, you should hear the start of the verse from "The Rain."

Congratulations on a great blend! Taking into consideration the bar structure of songs and using that to know *when* to blend makes for more musical and sonically pleasing DJing. Nothing is worse than rapping or singing along to a verse or chorus and then having the DJ cut it off right in the middle out of nowhere.

BLENDING OUTSIDE THE BOX

As you progress, you'll be able to blend songs a lot more quickly. That is, you'll be able to tell if the song you have cued up is too fast, too slow, or the same tempo. Also, you'll be able to blend smaller sections of songs that are connected. Maybe there are two songs with the same phrase that you want to mix or short instrumental breakdowns that sound good together. Try them all. Just keep in mind that you should have a plan and purpose with every mix. Know exactly what you want to do beforehand and practice it.

Keeping with the old throwback hip-hop theme, let's use DMX's "Party Up" and Blacksheep's "The Choice Is Yours (Revisited)" as our examples for blending outside of the box.

"The Choice Is Yours" is famous for the 4-bar bridge after the second chorus. Take a listen if you have it in your library or pull it up on YouTube.

It is not only a break from the standard chorus and verses of the song but also adds an unexpected, energetic build-up. We can also use this section as a transition point into a new song. That's where DMX's "Party Up" comes into play.

"Party Up" is a very hype and energetic song, and it just so happens to be close in BPM to "The Choice Is Yours (Revisited)." Furthermore, it has a 4-bar instrumental intro that builds up in energy.

So, if you're playing "The Choice Is Yours," once you reach that 4-bar bridge, play "Party Up" on beat and in sync from the first downbeat. You'll then have two very energetic parts of different songs playing at the same time. And when the bridge of "The Choice Is Yours" is done, the first chorus of "Party Up" will come right in.

This blend is connected not only by BPM, but also by bar length, genre, and more importantly, style, energy level, and overall vibe of the music. They won't all be as unique as this one, but this is how you take your blends to the next level.

TRANSITION TIPS

- Always have a plan when you're going to transition *in* and *out* of every song you play. A good DJ would think, "At the second chorus, I'll start the blend with the next song's intro," rather than, "I'll bring in this new song whenever it feels right."

- Don't try to blend songs that have very different BPM. Blending an 80 BPM song with an 85 BPM song will generally sound OK, especially if you "meet in the middle" by adjusting their pitches to put them both around 82 or 83 BPM. But trying to blend an 80 BPM song with a 100 BPM song will make both songs sound very bad. One song will be way too fast or way too slow. Yes, the technology is available to do this, but just because you *can*, doesn't mean you *should*.

- Don't cut off a song in the middle of a verse or chorus, especially if the crowd is singing along.

- Make sure your volume levels stay consistent during your transitions and with each song.

- Another way to keep volume levels consistent when blending is to swap the basses during the blend. Clashing basslines can make for a bad-sounding mix. So with the song that's cued up, turn the bass all the way down. Then, during the blend, simultaneously turn the bass of the song playing down and turn the bass of the song coming in back up to its original point. This is an advanced technique, so it will take more time to learn.

- Incorporate scratches when bringing in a song to add creativity and style.

BEAT JUGGLING 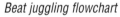 (28:17–end)

Beat juggling is the skill of replaying a section of a single song back and forth on the left and right deck. So while the song is playing on one deck, you have to spinback the same song on the other deck at the same time and play it on beat. This technique has roots to the very beginning of hip-hop DJing. DJs would play the breakdown section of a song repeatedly to give dancers at the party time to show off their skills. This is where the term "break dancer" comes from.

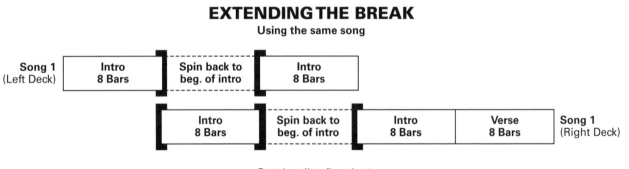

Beat juggling flowchart

Beat juggling can be done automatically using the Loop feature in Serato DJ, but try it manually first. Since you already have Missy Elliott's "The Rain" in your library, you can use that song (or any song with an 8-bar intro). In this example, you're going to play the 8-bar intro repeatedly. Here's how to do it:

1. Load "The Rain" on both the left and right decks and cue both sides to the first downbeat.

2. With the crossfader all the way to the left, hit play on the left side.

3. Let the first eight bars play. While it's playing, begin baby scratching the downbeat on the right side, on beat and in sync with the left.

4. When the 8-bar intro is finished on the left, let go of the right deck on the "one" and move the crossfader all the way to the right side. The intro of "The Rain" should now be playing on the right side.

5. Quickly spinback the left deck to the beginning and baby scratch on beat and in sync with the right. Use the headphones to do this so the sound of the record being spun back isn't heard.

6. When the 8-bar intro on the right side is completely finished, let go of the left deck on the "one" and move the crossfader all the way to the left.

7. Keep going from left to right as many times as you need to get the technique down, and more importantly, to get it *on beat*.

SHORTENING THE JUGGLE

Eight-bar juggles are great, but you can juggle even shorter sections of songs down to just one bar or even a couple of beats. When performing juggles that short, you'll need to pay attention to the amount of times the deck spins instead of using the headphones. Let's try this by performing a juggle with the first two bars of Missy Elliot's "The Rain."

Prepare the Juggle

The first thing you need to do is prepare the juggle by loading "The Rain" on both the left and right decks and cueing both to the first downbeat. Now, look at the orientation of your decks. More than likely, they are not oriented the same way, so you need to fix that.

If you're using vinyl, you can place a sticker or put a marking at the top of the record label. If you're using Serato DJ with a DJ controller that has a jogwheel, set a cue point at the first downbeat, and when you hit the cue point, the jogwheel light will orient itself straight up. If you're using Serato DJ with vinyl, set a cue point at this first downbeat, rotate both Serato records so the Serato label is facing up, and then hit the cue point you just set. At this point, both the left and right deck should be oriented facing up, and "The Rain" will be at the first downbeat. This is important because you need to know *visually* how far along you are in the song when you're juggling.

Orienting your decks to the downbeat using a sticker or marker on vinyl

Orienting your decks to the downbeat using a jogwheel

Orienting your decks by setting cue points in Serato

Orienting your decks to the downbeat using Serato records

See the Juggle

Your next step is to watch how many rotations your deck makes during those two bars. So hit play on the left side and count how many times the deck rotates while those two bars play. It should be a little bit over three rotations. So this means that when you play one side and switch to the other, you'll have to spin the first side back three times and orient the deck facing up to get back to the beginning. Now that you know this, you won't need headphones to cue up the song because you can see it.

Let's give it a try:

1. With the crossfader all the way to the left, play the first two bars on the left side.

2. When they are finished, let go of the right deck on the "one" and move the crossfader all the way to the right side.

3. While the right side is playing, quickly spin the left deck back three rotations and orient it facing up.

4. When the two bars are finished on the right side, let go of the left deck and move the crossfader all the way to the left.

5. Repeat these steps as many times as you need to get it down and on beat.

If done correctly, you should keep hearing the first two bars of "The Rain" via a seamless transition between the two decks. Once you get the hang of it, try juggles of different lengths by paying attention to the number of rotations that occur within the given bar count. For example, since two bars of "The Rain" take up just over three rotations, one bar should only be about one and a half rotations, and four bars should be just over six rotations.

CHAPTER 7: BUILDING A SET

Now that you've learned the basic skills of DJing, next is learning how to put *all* of that together to build a DJ set. At first, most of your sets will probably be planned ahead of time with you knowing exactly what order you'll play your songs. But as you gain more experience, you'll be able to DJ on the fly and play more free-form.

In general, you should prepare at least one song per minute for your sets. So if you're scheduled to DJ for an hour, prepare 60 songs. You won't play all 60, but you'll at least have options if you need to change things on the fly. And if you're asked to play longer, you'll already have prepared plenty of songs to choose from. For example, if you're DJing a '90s R&B party, and you have 20 songs prepared for a two-hour set, you won't have enough music. And the last thing you want to do is play the same songs over again during your set.

So, the first thing you need to think of is what type of event you're DJing—whether it's all new Top 40 hits, an '80s rock theme, or a techno night—because that will determine what music you play, what music you *don't* play, and how to best organize it.

CREATING PLAYLISTS OR "CRATES"

The best way to group your songs is to make playlists (or *crates*, in Serato DJ). These will be based on what makes sense to you and what fits your style. Your playlists are there to assist in quickly finding the music you want to play and to give ideas while you're scrolling through songs. Playlists can contain as many or as few songs as you want, as long as they help you find the songs you need when you need them.

Everyone organizes playlists differently, but here are some easy ways to start:

Genre: Create playlists based on the genres of music, like underground hip-hop, old-school rock, funk, R&B, house, techno, slow jams, and others.

Decade: Organize music around the decade it came out, like '90s party, '70s funk, '70s rock, '80s funk, '90s R&B, 2000s pop, 2000s rap, and so forth.

Energy Levels: Base playlists on musical energy level. Similarly, you can also organize it by imagining when you would play the song during an event:

- At the beginning of the party when people are just showing up

- As the party gets busy and is filling up

- When it's a full-on party and everyone is dancing

- When it's time to leave, and you need to slow things down

Venue/Event Type: Make playlists centered on the type of event or venue, such as weddings, school dances, bottle-service clubs, corner bars, backyard BBQs, and so on.

Theme Nights: This is more for specialized events like Halloween music, Valentine's Day, graduation music, etc.

Your Favorite Jams: To me, this is the most important playlist. Always keep a list or two filled with music that *you* love. It can be super hype or chill, it doesn't matter. Just keep it focused on your love and passion for the music.

Nothing at All: More experienced DJs many not have any playlists at all and will just DJ on the fly for their entire gig. But it takes years of experience and a large music collection to get to this point.

ORDERING MUSIC

Now that you've got playlists created or a group of songs ready to go, you need to figure out the *order* in which you want to play the music. Here is a list of tips to help you do that.

- Order the songs by BPM and blend each song starting from lowest to highest BPM.

- Listen to the intros and outros of songs and see which ones have certain connections that make sense. Maybe a musical phrase or song lyrics of one song will go well over the intro of a different song.

- Mixing "in key" is an advanced technique that takes into account the key of each song. So when you're blending and have two songs playing on top of each other, sonically it sounds pleasing. When Serato DJ analyzes your songs, it determines the key of each song, so use that as a tool to assist you.

- "Chunking Songs" is an organizing technique where you group four or five songs that you know sound good together and play them in a specific order. An example of a good chunk of songs for a hip-hop throwback party might be:

  - DJ Unk "Walk It Out" (80 BPM)

  - Lil Jon "Snap Yo Fingers" (82 BPM)

  - Cali Swag District "Teach Me How to Dougie" (85 BPM)

  - Yung Joc "It's Goin' Down" (85 BPM)

These are all hip-hop songs that were released within five years of each other, they have specific dance moves related to them, and they have very similar tempos. This strings together so many different attributes of the individual songs and makes for a great mix.

RECORDING YOURSELF

There is no better way to know if you're DJing correctly than to listen to yourself mix, and the best way to do this is to record yourself while DJing. You can connect a recording device to your DJ mixer to do this or use the recording feature on your smart phone and place it near your speaker. Even easier, Serato DJ lets you record your sets right inside the software.

Just hit the REC button on the top left of the screen to open the Record Window, make sure the Record Input Selector is set to "Mix," and hit the REC button to start recording.

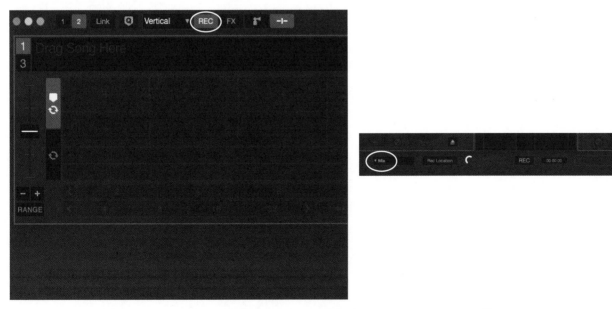

Use the Record buttons in Serato DJ to record yourself

Once you're done DJing, give your mix a name and hit "Save." A new playlist called "Recorded" will appear in the Playlist Window with the audio file of your mix in it.

When listening back to your mix, pay attention to the following:

- **Song Selection:** How did you feel about the songs you chose and the order you put them in?

- **Transitions:** Were the transitions smooth? Did the blends sound good? Did you transition at the right part of the song?

- **Volume Levels:** Did the volume stay consistent throughout the entire mix or were some parts too loud or too quiet?

- **Extras:** Did you scratch, try a new transition, loop a certain part of a song, or add any extra creative elements in the mix? What would you do different next time?

These are the questions you'll need to ask yourself as you listen to your mixes *and* when you listen to other DJs. Always keep your ears open to learn new things and then try them out. Then record yourself as you practice to hear how you're doing.

CHAPTER 8: FINAL TIPS/EXTRA CREDIT

Congratulations on getting through this entire book! Hopefully this has helped you learn the basics of DJing and inspired you to progress even further. Below are some final tips to guide you on your way.

DJing YOUR FIRST EVENT

When you finally get your first gig, *show up early.* Get there at least 90 minutes prior to the start time to set up your gear, perform a sound check, organize all your gear/cables so your setup looks clean, and get comfortable in your space. Do this for *all* of your gigs.

Pay attention to the crowd and energy levels of your music. Don't blast them with the biggest and most energetic songs right at the beginning, especially if you're opening up for another DJ. Build up the energy and pace yourself throughout the night. And keep your volume levels consistent as you transition between songs.

Reminder: Prepare at least one song per minute for your set. So if you're scheduled to DJ for an hour, prepare 60 songs. You won't play all 60, but you'll at least have some options if you need to adjust your set.

USING THE MICROPHONE

Some events will require you to host, which means talking on the microphone. Even if it's not required, you may want to do so anyway, so you can engage with the crowd. The best way to get comfortable with this is to just try it. Buy a microphone, connect it to your DJ gear, and have fun. Just remember to use discretion and get on the mic sparingly during your set. If you overdo it, you'll annoy your audience.

FINDING & DOWNLOADING MUSIC

Most DJs use a record pool to find music. In the past, these were services that would mail you vinyl records or CDs, but now they are mostly all digital. Record pools require a monthly subscription fee that will give you access to their library of music. They offer different versions of songs (clean, dirty, instrumental, intro versions, a capellas), exclusive remixes, and access to certain songs not made available to the general public. These are great because you not only get access to tons of music, but the quality of the audio files are usually the highest possible. Popular record pool websites are *DJcity.com*, *BPMSupreme.com*, *ClubKillers.com*, and *BeatJunkies.com*.

Yes, it's possible to download music from YouTube, SoundCloud, or other websites, but oftentimes the sound quality of those files is poor. Playing songs with low audio quality on a big sound system just makes you look (and sound) bad, so you should aim to have only WAV files or 320 KBPS MP3 audio files.

GO SEE OTHER DJs

Get out of your comfort zone and go see all the different types of DJs performing in your city and beyond. It not only helps people in the music scene get to know you, but also gives you the opportunity to learn new skills by just watching other DJs perform. Also, it's great to connect with other DJs to make the DJ community stronger.

VERSATILITY WITH EQUIPMENT & MUSIC

Sometimes you'll end up DJing gigs with DJ gear you're not familiar with. For example, if you're opening for another DJ, everyone performing before them may be required to use their setup so there's no down time between acts. You'll just have to figure it out. Make it easier on yourself by learning how to DJ with as much different gear as you can get your hands on. Also, sometimes you may have to play music you're not familiar with, so spend time learning about all different types of music to better prepare yourself for those moments.

PRACTICE. PRACTICE. PRACTICE.

The only way you're going to get better is by practicing at home—your transitions, blending, scratching, and juggling. Keep your music updated and organized, and be a master of your equipment. Make sure you know the ins and outs of every single knob, fader, and feature your DJ gear has to offer. This includes the DJ software you're using, like Serato DJ. Use the tutorials, keyboard shortcuts, and training materials included to learn every single feature, effect, and anything else that you can use to your advantage and become the best DJ you can be.

FIND YOUR OWN STYLE—BE UNIQUE

You can give multiple DJs the same set of songs, and they will all play them in a different way. Find what way makes sense for you and build on that. Maybe you like to scratch over the breaks of songs. Maybe you do interesting transitions between songs that no one else is doing. Or, maybe you're known for playing music no one else plays. Find *you* and *be you*.

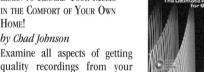

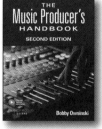